£4-50

CU00735078

MASTER
class

Golf

MASTER class
Golf

PETER D. SMITH

ANAYA PUBLISHERS LTD
LONDON

First published in Great Britain in 1993 by
ANAYA PUBLISHERS LTD
Strode House, 44-50 Osnaburgh Street, London NW1 3ND

Copyright © Anaya Publishers Ltd 1993

Managing Editor Masterclass Design Limited
Photographer Mark Newcombe, Visions in Golf
Designer Roger Daniels
Illustrations Ken Lewis & Masterclass Design Studio

British Library Cataloguing in Publication Data
Smith, Peter D.
Master Class Golf
I. Title
796.352

ISBN 1-85470-168-1

Typeset by Art Photoset Limited, Beaconsfield, Bucks.
Colour reproduction by J. Film Process, Singapore
Printed and bound in Italy by Officine de Agostini Spa, Novara

Thank You

I would like to express my sincere thanks to the following for
their help in the production of this book:-
For the supply of golf clubs, bag, and other equipment,

MacGregor Golf International, Paddock Road, Reading, RG4
0BY, and in particular to Philip Morley, Managing Director;

Clothing by **Glenmuir Ltd**;

Rainproof clothing by **Sunderland of Scotland Ltd**;

Footwear by **Etonic;**

Chill-proof jacket by **Mister Fox;**

Bill Reid, Wisley Golf Club;

La Manga Club, Spain, for their assistance and hospitality as a
venue for the photographs, and in particular the Director of
Golf, John Weir.

Contents

Introduction

Golf is often made out to be a very difficult game. It is not. It is surprisingly easy once you fully understand a few basic facts and have mastered a few simple movements.

Many golf books try to make the game sound terribly complicated as well as highly technical, yet for the average golfer the game should be relatively simple and, above all, enjoyable. There is no magic formula that will instantly make you a better golfer, nor any well-guarded secrets known only to top professionals.

For many years now I have been fortunate to work with some of the world's top teaching and playing professionals. Over the years their expertise has helped countless golfers, of all standards, from beginners to champions.

In this series of lessons you, too, can benefit from their help and skill, as I have concentrated their teachings into this series of lessons. You will learn not only how easy golf could be, with a little effort on your part, but also how to put the skills you will acquire to good use on the course. The aim of this book is not to give you a perfect, mechanical swing. I won't try to teach you how to swing like Nick Faldo, simply because you are not Nick Faldo. You must learn to play to the best of *your* ability, using the skills you acquire in the best possible way, never taking risks but always playing shots you know you can hit.

The one aim of this book is to bring your scores down.

The newcomer to golf will find everything he or she needs to know about playing the game. The more experienced player too, who seriously wants to improve, will find it all in this series of lessons. I strongly urge everyone to read each section fully as even the more experienced golfer will find the revision of the essentials will cut several strokes off each round.

A quick note of apology to left-handed golfers. The photographs and text all refer to right-handed players and it is not possible within the space we have to repeat everything with the reversal of "left" and "right". I hope the inconvenience of reversing sides will not affect your enjoyment of, and benefit from, this course.

I may also have used the male gender "he" or "his" in certain places. To all the many fine women golfers there are, again my apologies for not always including "she" or "her". It is purely a matter of space, not a sign of any disrespect.

Learning from this book and then practising will bring your scores down. Scoring better makes your golf even more enjoyable.

Hit it Straight — The Essential Ingredients

Every golfer wants to be able to hit the ball straight, or at least towards a definable target. To do so on a consistent basis, you will need the correct alignment, grip and stance.

Something like 80% of the faults in golf can be traced back to poor alignment, grip and set up, things you do before you even begin to swing the club. Get these right and you will have cut out 80% of your golfing problems.

I am going to show you the way to get into the best position to swing the club on a consistent basis and I shall deal with the process in exactly the same way as every professional would. Don't run away with the idea that this section is only for those who have never played golf, as it contains vital information for every golfer, of whatever standard. Even experienced golfers need to go back time and time again to the essentials, checking and rechecking them.

Only by getting these right will you be able to hit the ball well on a consistent basis. That will lower your scores substantially.

Alignment
What do you do when you want to hit a shot? Next time you are on the golf course make a mental note of your exact routine. I guarantee it is normally different from that of a professional.

What do they do? First, they look carefully at the lie of the ball, then calculate (normally with help from their caddy) how long the shot is to their target, whether that is the green or some other point on the course. They then decide what type of shot they need to hit, high, low, a fade or a draw; then and only then do they prepare to play the ball.

To do this they stand behind the ball, looking down the target line; then they move to the side of the ball, place the club head just behind the ball, adjusting it until it is square to the target line. Then they take their grip and get their stance right.

Just by reading this you can tell that the professionals take considerably longer than the average golfer at setting up before they hit a ball. The extra care they take is reflected in the greater accuracy they achieve. Forget the distance factor — professionals *do* hit the ball further than most club golfers. What is important is their degree of accuracy. How do they get it?

The answer is very simple. They line up better and take their grip very carefully as well as deciding exactly what type of shot they want to play.

In the example above — which you can watch on television or at any tournament — the sequence of events before a professional hits the ball is important and this is the way you must approach your golf if you are to play better. It is the only way to play.

It should become habit to align the club face and the body before taking the grip. Then, when the

Ian Woosnam proves that you don't have to be tall to power a golf ball.

About 80% of the problems in golf are caused by poor grip, stance and alignment

If you get these right you stand a better chance of playing good golf

Professionals line up to the shot better

Aim the club face where you want the ball to go

Be precise as a tiny error in alignment can cause a big error over 200 yards

You need to imagine a line from the ball to the target

grip is in place you are ready to play the shot. There is much you can do before you hit the ball, though not much after you have hit it to change its direction.

We start with the things you need to do **before** you swing.

You obviously need to know how long the shot is and what type of shot to play, but we shall return to that later. For now, just use a 7-iron and imagine you are faced with an easy, straight shot of about 135 yards, though if you hit a 7-iron less than this, don't worry.

Your first task, even before you take your grip, is to align the club face. If you are firing a gun or an arrow, playing snooker or bowling, you need to take aim first. It's the same with golf. Aim the club face in the right direction and you have a good chance of hitting the ball to your target.

In golf it has been shown that a 1° error in aligning the club will result in the ball being almost four yards off line at 200 yards. You can see from the illustration (below) that with a 3° error in alignment you would hit the ball 12 yards off

3°

A 3° error in alignment at address can cause you to hit the ball 12 yards off course.
Be precise.

line. That could put it in the rough or in a bunker.

You will notice that the professionals stand behind the ball before they begin their alignment. They do this to be able to look from here directly down the line to their target. They often look for a small mark on the ground just ahead of the ball — a leaf or twig, or perhaps a patch of grass that is a slightly different colour — to use as a direction finder. This is perfectly legal under the rules of golf. Choose something no more than a yard or two away as it is easier to align yourself with something very close rather than 200 yards away. You cannot, though, place anything on your line to help you on the course, though on the practice area it may help you.

Once you can "see" an imaginary line from the ball to the target, place the club head on the ground a half inch behind the ball, with the

A novel way of seeing if the club face is perfectly aligned is to stick a tee-peg to the face. It should point at the heart of the ball and on to the target.

club face square to your target.

One novel little way of telling if the club is correctly aligned is to fix a tee peg to the face of the club, fastening the top end of the peg to the club with a re-useable adhesive. The tip of the tee-peg should then point straight at the middle of the ball. When the club head is in position move to the side of the ball to take up your stance.

For the purposes of this exercise we shall use extra clubs laid on the ground as aids to taking aim. On the practice ground use these to help you — it will quickly build up your confidence in lining up. The photographs show this clearly. It is normally easier to use the bottom groove on the club face as your guide.

Once the club face is aligned you are ready to get your body alignment correct. We shall, later in this course, deal with shaping shots which can entail altering the stance slightly, but for now our prime concern is to be able to hit the ball straight. You must, therefore, align your club absolutely square to the target.

On the ground parallel to the club marking the line from ball to target, lay another club, about three feet away from the first club. This will show you the line for your feet. Adjust it closer to the first club if needs be. You then align your shoulders.

Hold another club across your chest. It should be parallel to the club laying across your toes. If not, turn your shoulders very slightly until it is.

You are now totally square to the target and thus perfectly aligned. You are now halfway to hitting the ball straight.

Lay some clubs on the ground to help you with your alignment. This will help train your eyes, making it easier for you once you are out on the course.

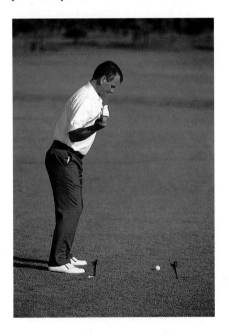

Hold another club across your shoulders, parallel to the club across your feet. You are now aligned.

Align your feet to the target line

You must also get your shoulders perfectly aligned, something many golfers get wrong

11

Your grip must allow you to
have feeling in your hands so
that you can control the shot

Any time your shots become
erratic, come back to the grip
and get it right

Your Grip
Once the club face and body are
aligned you take your grip, though
be careful not to move the club
head out of position.

The most widely used grip is the
one popularised by the great Jersey
professional Harry Vardon.
Although he did not invent the grip
his success in winning the British
Open six times between 1896 and
1914 (a feat never equalled)
focused attention on his technique.
Consequently most golfers adapted
their grips to the one he used. It is
a tribute to that fine man that it has
become known as the **Vardon
grip**.

Basically it has the little finger of
the right hand overlapping the
valley formed by the index and
middle fingers of the left hand, as
the photograph clearly shows. It is
also often referred to as the
overlapping grip.

There are a couple of variations
which have evolved over the years.
One, known as the "interlocking"
grip, has been very successfully
used by Jack Nicklaus and has the
little finger of the right hand
interlocking with the index finger
of the left. It can be of benefit to
players with short fingers. The great
Ben Hogan used a similar grip.

The other grip is the ten finger
grip, sometimes referred to as the
"baseball" grip, and this is
particularly useful if you have small
hands. Many younger golfers and
women use this grip. With this grip
it is particularly important to
ensure that there is no gap
between the two hands — they
must form a single unit.

Whichever grip you may feel
comfortable with, the point to
understand is that the hands must
form a single unit — if they are not

firmly connected they may work
independently, creating all sorts of
problems in your swing.

Take your grip with your left
hand first. The club should lay
across your left hand from the
"heel" — the pad opposite the base
of the thumb — to the first joint of
the index finger. Leave about half
an inch of the club overhanging the
end of the hand; this helps you to
control the club better and will
stop your glove wearing out.

The fingers then close around
the club. With the club head on the
ground the left thumb should be
very slightly to the right of the
centre of the shaft. If you have your
thumb straight down the centre of
the shaft, loosen the grip, turn
your hand very slightly to the right
and re-grip. You should be able to
see two knuckles on your left hand
but as this can sometimes be
difficult when looking down you
may find it easier to hold the club
upright, as shown. Make sure you
put it down square though,
rechecking your aim. Another good
check point is that, if you have
gripped correctly, the back of your
left hand (use the logo on the
glove as a guide) should be aiming
directly towards the target.

You should also be able to see
that the two middle fingers are just
touching the pad at the base of the
thumb. If they don't touch you
might need to have smaller grips
fitted to your clubs, or you should
grip down the shaft a little until
they do just touch. If they overlap
the thumb pad you might need
larger grips fitted. Ask your club
professional to check this for you if
you are in doubt.

The right hand is then placed in
position. Here, the club does not
lie across the hand so much but is

Right For people with smaller hands the ten finger grip can be suitable, but the hands must be kept close together.

Below The most widely used grip is the Vardon, or overlapping grip.

Below right The interlocking grip has been used by Nicklaus to great effect.

You should normally be able to see two knuckles on your left hand as you look down

Golf gloves come in different sizes — so do golf grips

The thumb on the left hand should be just right of the centre of the grip as you look down

The joint between your thumb and the forefinger on the right hand should be squeezed together, the forefinger being triggered for better control

 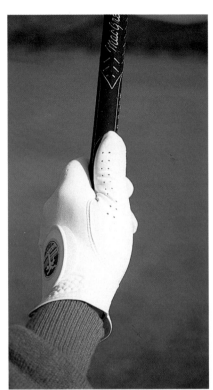

Hold the club firmly but don't strangle it

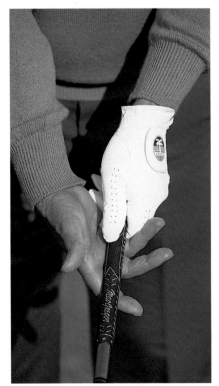 

Opposite, top left Leave about half an inch overlapping the hand. This gives more control.

Opposite, top right It is easier to see the two knuckles on your left hand if you hold the club upright in front of you.

Above Your two middle fingers should just touch the thumb pad as you grip the club. If they don't, ask your professional to check your grip size.

Opposite, bottom left The right hand grip is more in the fingers, with the index finger forming a trigger to give more control.

Opposite, bottom right Both the "V"s formed by the thumb and first finger should be pointing at the same spot, between the chin and right shoulder.

gripped more at the point where the fingers meet the palm, right at the base of the fingers. You must never grip the club in the palm of your right hand.

Wrap the middle two fingers around the club with the little finger overlapping the valley between the index and middle fingers of the left hand. The index finger of the right hand then wraps around the club but with a small gap between it and the middle finger. This is often referred to as the "trigger".

The joint of the right thumb and first finger squeezes together rather than being wide open.

If you use a grip other than the Vardon the only difference from any of the above is the position of the little finger of the right hand. Apart from that, nothing else in the entire set up or swing changes.

Your hands should now fit together snugly as a single unit. The left thumb is covered by the thumb pad of the right hand and, importantly, the "V"s formed by the joints of thumbs and first fingers should be pointing in the same direction, ideally towards a point midway between the chin and the right shoulder.

Many newcomers to golf — and a fairly large number of those who have been playing the game for several years — have what is termed a "strong" grip, the hands turned too far to the right. This can often cause a hook, unlike the "weak" grip where, with the hands turned too far left, you risk slicing the ball.

You can see these two positions, slightly exaggerated, over the page. Check your grip position in a mirror at home, where you can also practise taking your grip and setting your aim.

Many golfers have a very strong grip but this will stop you from releasing the hands through impact

You should practise taking your grip regularly, not just when you are at the golf course

This is a weak grip, the "V"s pointing at the left shoulder. This will cause a slice.

This is a strong grip, the "V"s pointing beyond the right shoulder. This would lead to a hook.

Go back to the grip regularly, checking it carefully before every shot

A tiny word too, about grip pressure. You need to hold the club firmly, so that it doesn't slip out of your hands as you swing, but you should not hold it so tight that you are strangling it. Hold it with the same pressure that you would use if you were holding a young child or a cat.

Far too many players grip the club as if they were about to strangle it. This is wrong and will result in poor shots. You do, of course, need to maintain control over the club and can't let it fly out of your hands once you swing it, but do relax your grip. If you ever want to check that you are not gripping too tightly, completely slacken off the pressure without removing your hands from the club, then slightly tighten them again. Feel that your hands are more relaxed.

The grip is something that needs fine tuning on a regular basis just like a high performance motor car. Having the grip slightly wrong will make all the difference between a good shot and a poor one. Take the time to get it right and constantly recheck it.

Whenever you hit a bad shot, go back to your grip and look at it carefully. There's a fifty-fifty chance that the shot was poor because of a faulty grip position. You will see professionals, whenever they hit a bad shot, replaying the shot — without a ball — to try to figure out what they did wrong. This is good practice, provided you know what you are looking for.

Opposite right Sandy Lyle went through a poor patch before bouncing back. If your game goes wrong come back to the essentials and work on getting them right.

At impact the club head must be in the same position as at address

Because we all swing slightly differently the ball position may vary slightly from player to player

Every golfer will find that their game goes slightly awry from time to time with shots being hit that are just not up to their normal standard. Every golfer goes through a poor patch now and again — even professionals; just think of Sandy Lyle who won the British Open and the US Masters, then had a couple of years of sheer misery before bouncing back. If you do have an off day don't go for drastic cures or try to change your swing. Go back to the beginning. Check your grip. Take your left hand grip and hold the club upright to see if you can see two knuckles.

Check that your "V"s are pointing to the correct place. Check that both your hands are perfectly aligned and that one is not drifting very slightly to one side.

Check your alignment too, to make sure you have been standing square to your target. Look in particular at your shoulder line as the shoulders and feet are often not quite properly aligned.

It pays to check and re-check the alignment and the grip. It takes very little time and you really should do it before every shot, just like the professionals.

The club hits the ball just before the bottom of the swing arc, which is why the ball will rise and spin.

If they consider it so important, even with their superior ball striking ability, it must be. You will play a better class of golf by following their example.

Never be afraid to return to this section — it is not a sign of weakness to go back to the essentials, but a sign of strength. If your grip and alignment are fine-tuned regularly, then you know that you will be able to play better golf more often. That must be worthwhile.

Addressing the Ball
The alignment and grip are the most important parts of the essential ingredients. We now move on to the address position, including the stance and ball position.

For an iron shot the ball should be played fractionally before the point where your swing reaches its nadir, with the club face square to the target.

The swing should bring the club head back into the same position every time. The thing to remember is that at impact the position of the club head should be exactly the same as it was at address. The ball needs to be in a position where you can comfortably get the club head square at the bottom of the swing arc every time.

Finding the exact ball position to suit your swing will take some time, as it varies from person to person, as does the swing itself.

Many teachers insist that the ball should be midway between the instep of your left foot and the centre of your stance, but I have to disagree with them slightly and tell you that it varies according to the shot and according to your swing pattern. That is dependent, to a degree, on your height and build.

Other teachers suggest that the

ball should be moved slightly back as the length of the shot decreases, the ball being furthest forward for the driver and furthest back for the wedge. There is far more validity to this suggestion and I would recommend you adopt this method,

I think you should slightly alter the ball position according to your shot. Obviously the longest club — the driver — puts the ball furthest from you, but it should also be further forward in your stance. Adjust the ball position according to *your* swing.

but only if it suits your swing pattern. I would stress that this holds good for normal shots from the fairway — at present we are not dealing with any problem shots or shots you wish to shape. Those we shall deal with later.

If you find you are topping the ball, or slicing it, try adjusting the position of your feet so that the ball is more in the centre of your stance. I would emphasise that this is for an iron shot; it changes slightly with a tee shot, but that is something we shall deal with later.

It is fairly obvious that, to hit a golf ball well, you need to be well balanced. In general your feet should be about shoulder width apart, wide enough to ensure you maintain your balance but not that wide that you risk swaying.

One quick way to find this is by walking! Suddenly stop, one foot a pace ahead of the other. Turn on your heels so that you are facing the front. Your feet are now the natural distance apart for you to make an athletic swing whilst remaining well balanced. Nature does it for you!

With your feet too far apart you will restrict your turn, tending to sway more. Put them too close together and you might lose your balance as you swing. Experiment with it until you feel comfortable.

One thing that newcomers find difficult is standing the correct distance from the ball. To some degree you will find this by trial and error, but if you stand too close to the ball you will swing more upright and possibly slice the ball; standing too far will cause you to swing flat and that could lead to a hook.

You can check by releasing one hand from the grip at

> You will find the perfect ball position for you by trial and error; vary the position until you find the one which is most suitable for you

> One perfect way to find your correct stance is to walk a few paces, stop, turn on your heels and you have the correct width of your stance

Above and above right To find the correct feet width for you, try walking! Stop, turn on your heels and you have the perfect stance, compliments of nature!

Opposite, far right The club should not be held too close to the body — about a hand's width from the thighs is ideal.

Right As you address the ball make sure that your right arm is not too far out in front of you as that will push your shoulders into an open position and cause a slice. Relax the right elbow more, holding it closer in to the side of the body.

Your right elbow needs to be tucked into the side of your body a little at address to stop you slicing

Leave a hand's width between the club and your legs to enable you to swing the club through properly

address and placing it between the club and your left thigh. This is a generalisation — don't measure it to the nearest millimetre! Feel comfortable.

One other vitally important ingredient in a good set up position is the way the arms hang when you are gripping the club. I see a great number of golfers who stand with their right arm too straight and held out too much in front. This pushes the right shoulder too high and forward, opening the shoulder line to the target and possibly causing a slice.

Good golfers stand with their right arm slightly more folded, and almost held in against their side. The fold of the right elbow — not the elbow bone itself — should be pointing about 45° left and forward, not directly left. This set up will help you to draw the ball, making you a better golfer.

Do beware, though, of holding it too close in to the body as that will restrict the flowing movement of the swing and you will lose the width of the swing.

The body at address can almost be divided into three; from the head to the hips; hips to knees; and knees to feet. Ideally, each of these three sections should be a straight line, but as we are not stick men this is not literally possible. Make sure you bend from the hips, *not* the waist.

Try to keep your spine as straight as possible, without becoming so rigid that you cannot turn. Your knees need to be flexed slightly. A large number of beginners stand with their legs too straight. This restricts the turn. You must remember to be athletically poised — not a statue.

You must keep your spine fairly straight rather than bending over the ball too much

---

Keep your knees comfortably flexed and hold your head up rather than letting your chin droop onto your chest

---

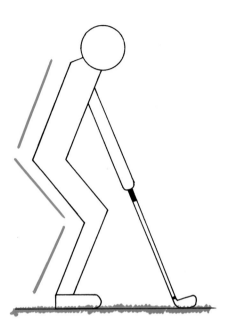

Try to keep your spine fairly straight, though not wooden. Try this simple exercise to see how upright you stand.

You will also see a number of golfers with their heads too low, their chins virtually resting on their chests. In this position the left shoulder, as you turn on the back swing, will knock the head out of position, and as one of the important points in golf is to keep the head fairly still, this immediately puts you at a disadvantage. Your head needs to be held erect enough for your arms to be able to swing through unhindered, and for your head to be able to remain fairly still. Too many golfers, having been urged to "keep your head down", do so at address.

Your chin must be comfortably held up as it is in normal, everyday life. Don't let it droop, but don't hold your nose in the air.

Never drop your head too much onto your chest as this will restrict your body turn.

The Swing

Now that we are fully in position, athletically poised and perfectly aligned, the next thing to do is to swing the club and hit the ball. The swing is often described in parts — the take-away, the back swing, the downswing and the follow-through.

Whilst it makes it more understandable to describe each part in detail, you must remember, when you come to swing the club, that it is just one flowing movement. For example, the take-away is merely the first part of the back swing; at the top of the back swing there is no pause before you launch into the downswing. Indeed, at the top of the back swing there is, in good players, a minute fraction of a second when the club is still being swung back, yet the body has started the downswing.

Don't let any of this confuse you. You will see how natural it is as we proceed. There are a couple of points about the swing you must understand. First, the back swing is a coiling motion, like winding up a spring. Think of one of those children's toys where you wind up a key and then release the toy, which scuttles away under its own power. The swing is like that. As you wind it up the key stays at the centre of the spring. The spring winds round the key. So it is with winding up the golf swing. The spring (in this case the arms and club) winds round the key (the body's pivot). A lot of golfers let the "key" move to one side — that is definitely wrong as we shall see a little later.

The swing is one smoothly flowing movement as Greg Norman demonstrates here effortlessly.

The body's pivot is an imaginary line from the head to a point midway between the feet. Basically it's a plumb-line from the head. Keeping your head firmly in place on the back swing will make you a much better golfer. The right leg plays a major part in this as we shall see, but remember — the spring coils round the key.

Before we begin swinging the club I want you to try a couple of very simple exercises.

Stand perfectly upright, your legs straight and your feet apart. Hold a golf club across your chest with your arms folded. Without moving your feet, but keeping your head as still as you can, turn your shoulders to the right until the club is pointing straight out in front of you. Hold that position and you should feel a stretching sensation in the back muscles.

Now turn to the left as far as you can go, though this time you can move your head so that you finish with your head and upper body facing the left. Also kick your right knee round so that it, too, is pointing at the target. Repeat the exercise half a dozen times until it feels fairly natural.

One more exercise before we swing the club. Place a golf umbrella in the ground and, as you stand, have your right leg pressed up against it. Now repeat the turning exercises a dozen times, stretching round to the right as far as you can go, but make sure you do not knock the umbrella out of the way. If you do knock it over you have swayed as you have turned right. That is one of the biggest faults in golf and one you must avoid at all costs.

Cast your mind back a few para-graphs to the child's toy and the

The swing is a coiling motion, rather like a child's wind-up toy; the spring winds round the key

To stop you swaying on the back swing, place an umbrella in the ground beside your right leg and avoid knocking it over as you swing back

Use this turning exercise before you begin playing as it will loosen up your muscles and allow you to turn with more freedom

Above and left Practise the golf turn by holding a club across your chest and turning as far to the right as you can, really stretching your back muscles, then turn to the left, turning to face the target as you do so. This is a wonderful exercise at the start of your round of golf.

Right To avoid swaying on the back swing place an umbrella in the ground by your right knee and swing; you should not knock it out of position.

Try to keep your left arm straight for the first part of the back swing

Forget about cocking the wrists — it is something which happens naturally

Turn your shoulders fully in the back swing

key. I said that the spring coils around the key, but that the key does not move out of position. The key is the body's pivot and the right knee is a major part of that pivot. You really must work very hard on keeping that right knee firm in the back swing. Not straight, firm. It is something we shall return to, but I would strongly recommend that, every time you play golf, or practise, you spend a couple of minutes doing this turning exercise. First it loosens the muscles and helps you stretch; second it reminds your muscles how to coil to build up the power of the golf swing.

Now back to the swing itself, with the club in position.

The first part of the swing is the take-away — that is, moving the club back from the ball as we begin to rotate the shoulders. There is a considerable amount of confusion over the take-away, mainly, I think, because too many golfers have, in the past, been told that it must be a "straight" take-away. It is not.

I am going to suggest here that you hold a club and, as you read this, enact the swing in very slow motion. It will help you to understand better the various ingredients of the swing that we have to put together later.

The swing begins with the arms and wrists held firmly — again, not rigid but firm enough that the "Y" formed by the club and arms does not change its shape for the first part of the back swing. The back swing starts with the shoulders rotating. Feel that you are pulling the right shoulder backwards. This automatically pulls the arms round and the club will follow. Be careful that you rotate the shoulders round the pivot — that plumb-line

down the back of the spine — rather than swaying to one side.

You must also avoid "picking the club up" on the take-away. That will produce too steep a swing, with a loss of power and direction in the shot.

A number of players, having in mind the "straight take-away" idea that has been mentioned in golf books before, move the club head back in a straight line. This can lead to what is known as an out-to-in swing on the way back down, the club head approaching the ball from outside the line.

As the right shoulder rotates backwards the arms follow it, bringing the club up and round. Keep the wrists firm at this point so that, if you suddenly stopped the swing, put the club head back on the ground where it is and turned your feet, you would be back in your address position.

Continue turning the shoulders. As you do so the arms are pulled back, as is the club. At some point the wrists will "cock", or hinge, but they will do this of their own accord, without you even having to think about it. A lot of golfers worry about getting the wrist-cock correct. Forget it — it happens on its own. Don't try to do it — don't try to stop it. Just swing the club.

As you swing the club back, your head should stay fairly still. I suggest, though, that you focus one eye firmly on the back of the ball, as doing something physical is simpler than thinking about something. Also, try to keep your left arm fairly straight so that you are extending the arc of the swing. That helps build up power.

Do make sure that you really turn your shoulders as far round as they can go, at least 90°, so that

The Swing Plane
To understand the swing plane better it might help to draw an imaginary line from the ball to the target, taking that line further back a couple of yards as well. You are standing inside that line and as you swing back the club will move inside that line. The downswing then brings the club down to the ball inside the line. At impact the club must be right on that line, to hit the ball squarely. It then moves along the line momentarily as it hits the ball before moving back inside the line again. This is referred to as an "in-to-in" swing pattern.

Some players swing the club outside the line on the way down to the ball, leading to either a slice or a pull left. This is called an "out-to-in" swing. There is also an "in-to-out" swing where the club approaches the ball from inside the line but then carries on going across it to outside. This can cause either a nasty hook or, more likely, a straight push to the right. Remember the "in-to-in" swing pattern and you will end up hitting more shots straight.

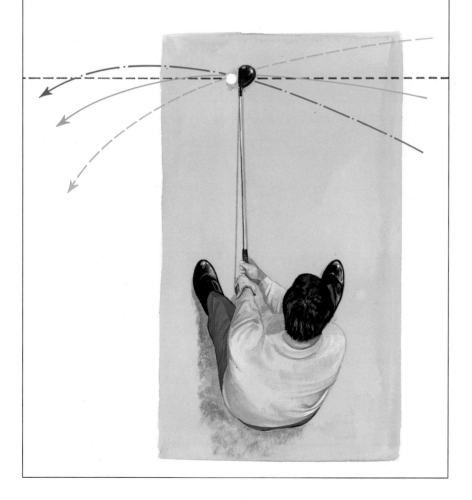

Keep your left foot on the
ground in the back swing; the
weight rolls to the inside of the
foot but don't raise your heel

As you swing back make sure
your left shoulder is well under
your chin, your back facing the
target

your back is facing the target. Keep one eye focused on the ball.

A number of golfers raise their left heel at this point. To be a really good golfer you should try to keep the left heel firmly on the ground, only rolling the left foot slightly onto its instep. If you find that difficult raise it only very slightly.

Your right leg must stay firmly flexed, just as at address. From that position, all it does is twist from the hip. You must not let it sway to one side or you will pull the entire pivot out of line. Remember our umbrella.

Don't, however, go the other way and let your right leg sway away from the umbrella. This is known as a reverse pivot and it, too, will cause you some major problems.

At the top of the back swing you should be feeling a stretching sensation in your back muscles. Your shoulders should have turned well through 90º, your hips about 45º, and the club should be virtually horizontal and pointing straight down your target line. You can't always see this for yourself, so get a friend to help you check it.

Make sure, though, that they fully understand what they are supposed to be looking for. Advice from some golfers, friendly and well meant though it might be, can sometimes make a poor position

At the top of the back swing the shoulders must have turned through 90° so that your back is facing the target. Keep your left heel on the ground.

The view from the front shows that the shoulders have completed their 90° turn, the head is still above the back of the ball and the hips have not swayed to the right.

worse. The best thing to do is either to use a mirror or to ask a golf professional to have a quick look at you.

Now for the downswing, and there is an ongoing debate about what starts this. Some say the legs, some the arms, some the shoulders; others the hips. With our wind-up toy, releasing the key and placing it on the floor starts the thing in motion.

The human body is not quite as mechanical as that and we need to do something to kick-start the downswing. As I said, opinions vary but the majority of more experienced golf professionals now suggest that it is the lateral movement

of the body weight towards the target that drives the swing. At the same time the hands pull down hard on the club and the hips turn out of the way to make room for the club to swing through. It is, though, all a matter of transferring the weight.

Think of a glass of water. If you hold it still but then suddenly move it to one side (the back swing), the water changes its level in the glass but would then find its natural level again if held still.

If you then swing it the other way (transferring the weight on the downswing) the water resists but then catches up again, coming back to level. The body weight does

The downswing begins with the transfer of weight to the left, the hips moving laterally and the hands pulling down hard on the club

Imagine you are pulling a bell rope

The turning of the hips, together with the lateral movement of the body weight to the left, kicks the downswing. The arms pull down hard on the club. At this point the hands are ahead of the club head.

Fractionally after impact you can see how the right arm has straightened, the hips have moved out of the way and the body weight has hit through the ball and is still transferring to the left. The head has stayed over the back of the ball until after impact.

A moment before impact the hands are still working overtime to get the club head back to that square position. You must, though, never try to hit "late". I would suggest, on the contrary, you try to hit early, making sure your left arm is straight at impact, as it was at address.

At impact the hands must have pulled the club face back square

The weight of the lower body moves left as you approach impact but you must keep your head behind the ball

At impact the arms and hands have returned the club to its square position, seen better in this picture with the driver.

Drive the club head through after impact, rather than trying to decelerate it quickly. As you finish you should be facing the target, your right knee having kicked round and your weight perfectly balanced.

The hips turn out of the way as you swing down to make room for the club to swing through; standing very slightly open helps this

exactly the same in the swing.

The back swing pulls the weight to one side of the body — though it turns rather than sways. Then it transfers to the left as you swing. The important point is that you move the glass first — the water catches up with it because at first it resists by flowing up the right side of the glass before the force of the glass moving makes it catch up and settle to level again.

Impact

Let's look, now, at what position we want to create at impact. The club face needs to be perfectly square to the target. To achieve that the arms need to swing down. To make room for them the hips need to be moved out of the way.

Let's start with the hips. At the top of the back swing they have turned through about 45°.

They are, though, still perfectly positioned over the pivot line. Although I have warned you against swaying on the back swing, the first movement on the downswing is a sideways sway of the hips to the left. They begin turning at the same time.

As this lateral movement of the hips towards the target begins you must pull the club down with your hands, just as if you were pulling down on a bell rope. You will remember that we have tried to keep the left arm as straight as possible throughout the back swing. You want to try to keep it fairly straight coming down as well. This increases the width of the swing arc and will give you more power.

As the arms begin pulling the club down your hips will rotate towards the left, the weight moving onto your left foot. Don't try to do

Drive through impact, imagining you have a second ball to hit another foot or so in front

You must get the hands working overtime as you approach impact to square the club face to the ball

At impact there is a straight line from your left shoulder to the club head; that straight line needs to be replicated at impact if you are to hit the ball straight

anything unnatural here — concentrate on moving the hips out of the way and keeping the left arm straight: the rest will follow.

As you approach the impact position your hips are ahead of the ball, yet your head is still behind it. Be careful, as you move your hips laterally, that you do not pull your head out of position. It must not move. Concentrate on focusing one eye on the ball and the head will remain fairly still.

At impact itself the biggest single fault of less experienced golfers is to have the club head trailing behind the hands. Look carefully at the photograph and you will see that the straight line we had at address, from the club head up through the shaft and right arm to the shoulder is almost exactly repeated at impact. This picture also clearly shows how the hips have moved out of position, but look very closely at the position of the hands. Compare it with the photograph where we are halfway down before impact. In that photograph the hands are still pulling the club down and the wrists are still cocked — there is no straight line from the shoulder to the club head.

Somewhere between the two positions shown, the wrists have to straighten the club to replicate the straight line we had at address. Inexperienced golfers can lack the strength and technique to do that, often leaving the club behind. That can cause a slice or a push right.

The wrists have to work overtime here to get the straight line at impact. You will recall that we also saw that at impact the club face has to be in the same position as it was at address — that is, square to the target. This is

possibly the hardest part of the golf swing and you will not master it immediately.

We shall go back over this in a few minutes.

After impact comes the matter of the follow-through and once again this is an often neglected part of the swing. Although you can do nothing after impact to change the direction of the ball you must be aware that the swing is one flowing movement and if you have performed the parts before impact correctly, you will finish in a certain position. If you finish out of position you will know that, somewhere in the swing, you have done something wrong. The ball will also tell you what you have done wrong by the way it flies (or doesn't!). In the advanced section later in this course we shall be looking at how you can use the flight of the ball to tell you what you have done wrong.

Getting to a good follow-through position is just proof that you have kept accelerating the club head through the impact zone, thus putting all your power into the shot. Had you slowed the club down before impact you would not have hit it hard enough. At impact the club head needs to be travelling at its maximum speed.

From the top of the back swing the club head picks up speed, being at maximum speed as it hits the ball. Thereafter it continues up into the finish position, but it must not be slowed down too early.

At impact the left arm is straight, but the right is slightly flexed at the elbow. Just after impact the right arm, too, straightens as the right hand begins rolling over the top of the left.

This is a difficult part to get right

but it is largely the way the hands work which allows professionals to hit the ball further.

We shall come back to this later in the course as we move on to discuss more advanced techniques, but if you can understand it here you will be on the right track.

One more thing you should do is to drive the club head down the target line after impact — just one more reason why you should not slow the club down at impact.

Imagine that you have a further target just a couple of feet ahead of the ball and that you need to hit this with the club head. As you can

To help you think about driving the club head through the impact zone imagine you have another club ahead of you, set into the ground. Your aim should be to hit the grip of this club as you continue your follow-through.

see from the photograph I have set another club in the ground. My aim, after having hit the ball, is to hit towards the grip of this club with the club I am swinging. That will help ensure that I am swinging straight down the line at impact, rather than aiming the club face off outside the line, or too far inside.

You almost get the impression,

with this exercise, that you are steering the shot. That is a good feeling to acquire and will result in you hitting a much higher proportion of straight shots.

After impact the body keeps rotating so that you finish facing the target. Your right knee has kicked round completely and your right foot is on tip-toe. Do make sure that when the right knee kicks it moves round to the left, towards the target, not out in front of you. That is a fault of many golfers and will lead to a loss of power. Whilst dealing with the legs, try to finish with your left leg reasonably straight; don't let it collapse.

You should finish upright and perfectly balanced.

Finally, a word about the speed of the swing. Bobby Jones once said that nobody has ever swung a club too slowly. Although he said that over 70 years ago when clubs were made of different material, it still holds good today. Most golfers try to swing too quickly, with a resultant loss of control. There is no definite speed at which you should swing. Everyone is different, some can swing much faster than others. Vijay Singh, the top Fijian golfer, swings the club through faster than Concorde. He can, though, control it.

Today's top professionals swing the club, from start to finish, in about 0.8 of a second. From the start of the take-away to the top of the back swing is about 0.6 of a second; from the top of the back

swing to the finish is about 0.2 of a second. You can clearly see from this just how important it is to have a slow, controlled back swing. The club does, after all, come to a stop at the top of the back swing before it begins its journey down towards the ball, so there really is no point in swinging back fast.

You and I cannot, and should not, swing the club too fast. To help you with your swing rhythm, particularly at the start of a round or practice session, swing two clubs together. This does two things. It helps to establish a good swing rhythm; and it also ensures that you get your hands moving well ahead of the club head on the downswing as well as forcing you to move your hips forward and out of the way as you swing through.

A lot of golfers think they will hit the ball further if they swing faster. Most of them won't. But try it next time you are at the driving range. Swing as fast as you possibly can. The results will probably be horrible, so you can quickly go back to establishing a **smooth** swing.

This, then, is the swing technique. It may sound a lot to learn for something that happens in less than a second, but it is the only thing you do in golf so you should take the time to learn it.

Nobody gets it right every time but if you understand what you should be doing and why, it might make it easier to get it right on a consistent basis.

Don't give up if, having read this, you go out and find that the ball is not going exactly where you planned. It takes the three "P"s — perseverance, practice and patience. But everyone can do it.

Vijay Singh, the popular Fijian golfer, has one of the fastest swings on the European Tour. If you ever get the chance, watch him, but don't try to mimic him or you might lose control. Swing to the best of *your* ability.

Many professionals will tell you that you have not hit the shot until you have finished the follow-through

You should finish with your body having turned to face the target, your right knee kicking round to the left and your right foot on tip-toe

Hit the Green!

Many golfers fail to get the ball onto the green with their second shot on some par-4s, either because they lack length on their tee shot or from the fairway, or because their approach shot is a little wayward.

To make par they need to get the ball very close with the next shot. This is why the short game is such a vital part of golf. I want to show you how to get the ball safely on the green every time on those short shots.

We have so far looked at the alignment, set up, grip and swing. We have been using something like a 7-iron for these exercises and I suggest that, for what we shall do now, you use the same club.

In a round of golf there are eighteen holes, four of which are normally par-3s. Of the remaining fourteen only about ten or twelve will require a driver. If your first aim in golf is to score 90 on a regular basis — and let me put that in its proper perspective by telling you that 80% of all golfers in the world never regularly score less than 90 — you will only use the driver about a dozen times in a round. By the way, break 90 regularly and you will be in the top 20% of golfers in the world. Think about it.

Although we are using only one club at the moment, all the short irons are used in basically the same way. In an average round of golf,

60% of all shots are played within 100 yards of the pin, so you will probably use the short irons about thirty-five times.

The short game requires pinpoint accuracy and perfectly struck shots every time. I am going to teach you two things. First, in this part of the course, how to get the ball safely on the green nine times out of ten, whether there are bunkers, lakes or anything else in the way.

In the second part of this course I shall show you how to hit close to the pin whenever it is reasonably safe to do so but, above all, to play within your capabilities. You will always be playing the nine-times-out-of-ten shot, not the shot of a lifetime.

We are going to start with a little chip shot, the sort we might encounter if we were about 40 yards from the flag with no bunkers or other hazards in the way. Once that is mastered we can move back to hit longer shots.

If you can learn to hit shots accurately 40 yards, you can hit them accurately 240 yards. A long shot is the same as a short shot with one variation — the arc of the swing is wider, not because you swing the club differently but because the club shaft is longer. If you can control the club head on a short shot you will be able to control it on a long shot.

For this exercise you will need to be at the practice area of your local golf course. Stick an umbrella in the ground about 60 yards away For a moment I want you to put the club aside, choose a new target about 20 yards away — I marked

Nick Faldo shows supreme control on this short shot to the green. It is the ability to get the ball close to the pin from these situations which sets up birdie opportunities — or saves a par!

Over 60% of the shots in golf are played from within 100 yards of the pin

If you can regularly break 90 you will be in the top 20% of golfers in the world

Once you learn to hit shots accurately 40 yards you can hit them accurately 240 yards

Have two targets — one about 20 yards away, the other at about 60 yards. Once you have mastered these exercises hit balls to each target alternately.

Throw a ball to a target 20 yards away. You will note that the "follow-through" is longer than the "back swing". Note also how the ball rolls towards the target once it lands.

As you swing the club you will notice a ratio of about 45/55 in the lengths of the back swing and follow-through. To increase the length of shot increase the length of swing.

A long shot is almost the same as a short one, with the exception that the swing is longer

There is a ratio between the back swing and the follow-through; it is normally in the region of 45/55

Even on a very short shot go through the routine af aligning the club, then your body and taking your grip

It does help to adopt a slightly open stance for shorter shots as that will give you room for the club to swing through

Ball position on short shots is vital; it should be further back

that one with the umbrella and the 60 yard target with a flag, as they show better in photographs — and throw a few golf balls underarm to land by it. Try six or seven until you can get them to land fairly close — within about two feet. As you throw them make a mental note of how far you draw your arm back and how far forward your arm goes as you release the ball.

Chances are the ratio back to through was in the region of 45:55. Now take the club again and try to swing it through with the same ratio — that is about 45% back; 55% through. You don't need to hit the ball yet.

At the finish the club should just come up to the horizontal. This is not a full "wind-it-round-your-neck" finish, but just a little push forward of the club, not much more than for a long putt, really.

Now let's set up correctly and play the shot, to the further target. Have the ball in the middle of your stance and stand slightly open to the target. We do this because, on a short shot, you do not have the same lower body movement as on a full shot. Therefore the hips do not rotate in the back swing by much, nor do they move out of the way on the downswing.

To compensate for this we need to move them out of the way in the beginning or we risk knocking our arms against our left leg as we play the shot. The other point about standing open to the target is that it restricts your back swing and, as we have seen, we only want a very short back swing.

An important note here about the ball being in the middle of the stance. In our first section I emphasised the importance of getting the right ball position to

suit your swing, suggesting that, to begin with, you had the ball in the middle of your stance and that you stand square to the target.

When we open the stance (don't confuse this with having your feet wider apart — we are talking about turning the body slightly to the left of the target) the ball immediately appears to be further back in the stance. This is particularly so on short shots and in some bunkers where we need to stand quite open to the target. Some golf books suggest that, on a short shot, the ball should be opposite your left instep. If you took this literally, aligning your body first and then positioning the ball, you would, in reality, have the ball so far forward that it would be way outside your left foot and very difficult to play.

Stand square first, get the ball positioned correctly to your **square** stance, then change the body alignment. The ball will **appear** to move **back** in your stance — that is exactly what you want. For a shot this short your feet should be fairly close together, but maintain your balance.

Because of this stance and ball position your hands will be slightly ahead of the ball, so that your wrists are already slightly hinged. The line from your left shoulder down through your arm and the club shaft should be virtually straight, though don't hold your arm ram-rod stiff, or get into an uncomfortable position. You must feel relaxed, not tense.

As you swing the club back your

If you stand square with the ball centrally in your stance, but then turn so that you are standing open, the ball appears to move back in your stance. Take a square stance first.

The great Christy O'Connor used to play short shots with the ball directly opposite his right foot, his hands well ahead of the ball. That way he was sure of always hitting down into the ball

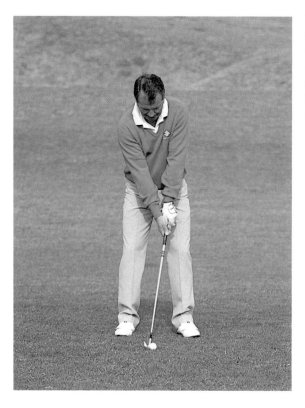

The ball here is fairly central, but note how there is an almost straight line from the left shoulder to the club head. You need the same straight line at impact.

Make sure you have that straight line from your left shoulder to the club head, at address and at impact

This is not quite a full back swing, the hands only just reaching the shoulders. The shoulders must turn, however.

At impact there is a straight line again from the left shoulder to the club head.

You should finish with the arms fairly straight in front of you. This helps restrict the length of shot. You do not need a full follow-through as this is not a full shot.

If you want the ball to stop fairly quickly once it lands do not release the hands going through, but finish with the back of the left hand still pointing at the sky

You really must accelerate the club through impact — never just swing limply at it

There is still some body turn as you hit the ball; you always finish facing the target

It is essential to keep your head behind the ball until after impact

wrists will cock slightly, but do guard against picking the club up steeply. Your wrists should stay reasonably firm so that the angle between your left arm and the shaft does not alter too much.

You also have to realise that the club head needs to be accelerating into the ball so you need to swing it back far enough to be able to produce enough speed at impact. Getting to know the exact length of back swing will take some time and practice.

Having decided on the length of swing you need, and keeping your wrists firmly held in that pre-set position relative to the arms, swing the club back and through. The slow back swing will help you to accelerate the club head through impact. That is vital on long shots but it is probably more important on short shots where you really must push the club head through impact, not slowing down at all. Remember, also, that you have 45% of your swing back, 55% through. To get the club that far through you *have* to accelerate from the top of the back swing.

As you come through impact keep the club head accelerating but keep the same angle between arm and shaft that you had at address. You should finish with the left arm and shaft in a straight line, as the photograph clearly shows. If that line is broken it is because you have flicked at the ball rather than hitting through it. You must get the feeling, in much of golf and particularly on short shots, that you are dragging the club head through with your left arm and wrist. To really understand this feeling you should practise short shots just using your left arm and hand. You will have to keep the left wrist fairly

firm to control the club head and your arm must stay firm if you are to hit the ball. Try it. Hitting 30 balls one-handed will help you to understand how the wrists work.

If you just take the club back and then limply swing it at the ball you will merely bounce the ball forward ineffectively. It must be a crisp shot into the back of the ball, with a longer follow-through than back swing. To control the shot you must keep the wrists firm, which will keep the club face on line and result in the shot going to the target. If you are not hitting it straight it is because you have changed the alignment of the club face between address and impact.

This is a very gentle shot, more like a long putt than a full swing and you need to stay as quiet as you possibly can. Basically, only the arms and shoulders swing — the body does not really move very much. Concentrate hard on keeping your head still and the rest of your body will stay "quiet".

Avoid trying to take the club back in a straight line, as that can cause an out-to-in swing and it would be exaggerated on this short shot, possibly causing a shank — the ball coming off the club face at the point where it joins the shaft (also called the socket). You swing the club back naturally on the body target line, not the ball to target line. Look carefully at the drawings opposite and you will see what I mean. You must not confuse the body target line with the ball target line. The club is always swung on the body target line, never on the ball-to-target line. It is inevitable that the club will move inside the line a little on the way back; it must happen, but don't try to pull it in too much, nor try to hold it straight. As your arms swing naturally the club will follow.

Getting the distance right on this type of shot will take some experimentation — it is not something you can learn from any book, you must experience it for yourself. Try it until you can land eight out of ten balls within five feet of the target. You will have noticed that, as the ball is not getting very high off the ground it will roll once it lands, even in fairway length grass. If you were playing to a green the shorter grass and smoother surface would make the ball run further, so you would need to adjust your shot to land on the edge of the green and roll to the hole. For now try to land the ball short of the target, possibly midway between you and the target so that it will roll.

The next stage is to hit the ball further. The action is the same, but the back swing is now longer in order to generate more power. Again, think of winding the toy up; the more you wind it the further it will go. Golf is the same — wind the swing up more and it will

release more power.

Stand a little more square this time, with the ball in the middle of your stance. Your hands are still slightly ahead of the ball so that you have begun the wrist-cock, so once again forget about this. There should again be an almost straight line from your left shoulder to the club head. Take the club back further, holding your head still above the ball and turning round the pivot. Don't sway. If you think you might, place another umbrella next to your right leg and avoid knocking it over.

As you take the club back further your wrists will automatically cock more — you don't have to worry about it, it's natural. Swing back about halfway, your hands coming up to just above shoulder-high and then through impact, again ensuring you accelerate through the impact position. You should finish much further through this time, the club reaching at least shoulder height. You will also be turning your shoulders more on the back swing and your body as you reach the follow-through

On short shots like these, the higher the ball goes, the less it will roll. If you want it to roll more, use a less lofted club and hit it just the same. It is the club which gets the ball airborne, not the swing

As the back swing lengthens your wrists will automatically cock

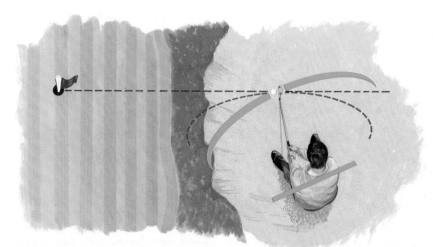

Make sure you always swing along the body line, not the ball to target line as that causes an in-to-out shot and a sharp hook.

position. At the finish there will be no straight line from your shoulder to the club head.

Earlier, in the section on hitting it straight, I suggested you should have the feeling of trying to steer the shot, driving the club head through the ball and on to a second target a couple of feet in front of you — we used a second club set into the ground, the shaft of which we were trying to hit on the follow-through.

It's worth reminding you of this now as you begin swinging a club and hitting the ball. We also need to go back to the swing path, where we saw that in-to-in would give you the best result. A number of players try to roll their hands too quickly as they hit the shot and end up pulling the club left too quickly. Feel that you are hitting through the ball, not at it.

As your swing develops you will increase the length of the shot simply by increasing the length of the back swing. Nothing else changes, apart from the set up becoming more square the further you hit the shot.

By now you should be hitting the 7-iron well over 100 yards and getting it reasonably straight. At present you are still only swinging three-quarters length, the club never reaching much more than vertical on the back swing.

Concentrate on keeping your head still and rotating your shoulders round that firm right knee on the back swing — avoid swaying; then on the down swing get your arms to straighten just before impact and then let the

This time, with 130 yards to the green and hitting a 7-iron I am standing just slightly open.

The professionals often try to fade the ball in on a short shot as that makes it stop better. Stand slightly open on short shots but still hit through the ball

Again, remember to keep your head behind the ball until after impact, though don't sway backwards on the back swing

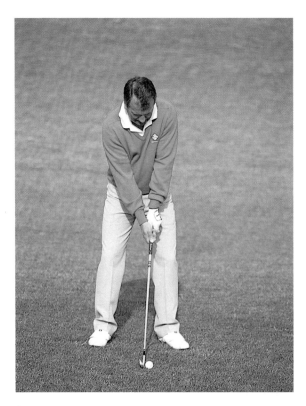

The ball is fairly central in my stance but once again there is a straight line from the left shoulder to the club head.

The back swing is longer, but still not full. Turn the shoulders more though.

At impact that straight
line we had at address is
replicated.

Not a full finish but turn
the body to face the
target as you keep
swinging through the
shot. Never quit.

straight right arm take control, pushing the club towards the target. As you continue turning the club will rise and finish past your shoulders.

One point I really must stress is that you began with that first little shot at a very sedate speed. As you increase the length of the back swing **the speed stays the same.** Don't believe that, as you increase the length of the back swing, you have to swing faster. The speed stays the same — slow but smooth.

A full swing with a 7-iron should hit the ball about 130-140 yards, but don't worry if you are not reaching that distance. Concentrate on getting a clean, firm, straight shot, the club coming down into the back of the ball and taking a divot — never try to lift the ball off the turf cleanly. Take a divot — it's the sign of a well-struck shot.

Any time your shots get out of control, come back to the essentials and hit short, 60-yard shots with the 7-iron. It will put you back on the right track.

You will also now find that the other lofted clubs in the bag, 8, 9 and wedge, become easy to use. They hit the ball less distance but higher, which is what they are made for. They are used to get the ball safely onto the green over bunkers, streams or any other hazards in front of the green.

Your set up on these short shots should always be the same. Have the ball in the middle of your stance, stand very slightly open to your target (more open the closer you are to the green) with your weight about 65% on your left foot, so that you are pressing the hands slightly ahead of the ball at all times. Take the club away smoothly, following your body line and try to

keep your head as still as you can, using your arms and shoulders more to generate the power you need, always remembering that 45:55 ratio for the swing. Always guard against swaying on the back swing. Concentrate only on getting the club face square to the target at impact and leave aside all other thoughts about weight transfer, wrist-cock and anything else.

It will pay you enormous dividends if you practise the short game consistently. Even at a driving range, where the temptation is to spend all the time hitting the driver, spend at least half your time with the shorter clubs, always aiming for a specific target. At your golf course you may find a practice area where you can hit over a bunker to a green. If not practise chipping the ball over your golf bag, using that as an imaginary hazard. Alter the distance now and then, starting with the 7-iron chip and run, then moving back to use the 9-iron, 8 and then the full swing with the 7-iron. Always aim for a specific target rather than just trying to hit as far as you can. Despite what it might seem, golf is not a matter of who can hit hardest, but of who can work the ball safely to the target.

Backspin
Much is heard about backspin these days and on televised golf tournaments we always see the professionals hitting shots to the

Seve Ballesteros and most other professionals use balata balls, but they do need to be hit perfectly if they are to spin back. Ironically, most amateur golfers need to hit further.

Never alter the speed of your swing on a full shot — maintain a smooth rhythm at all times

---

We all swing at different speeds. To find the one which suits you best, try hitting six balls with a very fast swing; six with a very slow swing and six with a medium swing. You will find one speed that suits you

Professionals have this knack of spinning the ball back once it lands on the green, but the average golfer hardly needs backspin as he is invariably short of the pin

If you want more backspin you could use a balata ball, though as they cut more easily they will end up costing you more

green which then spin back towards the hole — and sometimes back off the front of the green.

Whenever you hit a golf ball you spin it. If you hit it with side spin it will spin to one side — a slice or a hook. If you hit it with topspin, as you do a wood off the tee, it will travel further. On a shorter shot you want the ball to go straight but high. That needs backspin and every time you hit the ball straight with a short iron you hit it with backspin.

Almost every golfer wants to get his hands on the magic potion that is going to allow him to spin the ball back like the professionals, but few actually need it, as most golfers leave the ball short of the flag anyway. The vast majority need to hit the ball further so that it runs towards the pin. It is rare that the club golfer goes through the back of the green. And in truth there is no magic potion. Getting backspin on the ball only takes a perfectly hit shot and a balata ball.

The perfectly hit shot is one where the club face connects with the back of the ball as the club is still coming down. That squeezes the ball against the turf and puts backspin on it, causing it to rise quickly. You will do that as you improve.

Balata balls are more expensive than the normal surlyn covered balls that most people use; they also cut easier as they have softer covers. Professionals change their golf ball about every four holes as they mark or even split them. If you can afford five expensive, new golf balls a round, then fine. I consider I have done well if I get round with the one ball, not losing any on the way!

I think Ben Hogan explained

backspin better by calling it "underspin" — that is by hitting under the ball you put spin under it, making it rise faster and stop quicker once it lands.

What you will find as you improve is that, when you hit a ball very well, connecting at exactly the right point and hitting the ball straight, with no side spin, it will, once it hits the green, stop very quickly. This will only happen with the short irons, though, from about a 6-iron through to the sand wedge and particularly when the green is wet and soft. Don't expect to hit a 3-wood at the green and have it stop on landing. Not even Faldo can do that!

Getting it on the Green

At this point we are going to leave aside the technique of hitting the ball and look at the important mental side of golf, as it relates to short shots.

There will be many occasions on the golf course where you are faced with a shot to a green that is not straightforward. There may be a lake in the way, or a large bunker, or the green may be elevated so that you can only see the top of the flag. You might have mis-hit your approach shot and need to get the ball close to the pin to have a chance of saving par.

The instant you are faced with such a shot you put extra pressure on yourself. New golfers in particular have a terrible fear of hitting the ball over a lake or bunker and as they face up to the shot they are more tense than normal.

It's easy for me to tell you to just

Put a lake between you and the green and the shot becomes totally different.

54

ignore the water — forget it's even there. When you're standing on the edge of a lake or in front of a huge bunker, that's not a lot of help. You can't make the water disappear and closing your eyes won't do you much good either. The lake or bunker is there and will be for some good few years to come, unless there's a terrible drought or they alter the course.

What you should do is to look at it from a financial point of view. The golf ball has cost you something and if you lose it you will have to buy another. If you do have to buy another ball, will it ruin you? Is it a case of buy another golf ball or pay the mortgage? If the financial loss of this golf ball is going to affect you, give up golf.

If not, what are you worried about? On the practice range, or even on the course if there was no bunker or lake in the way, you would calmly hit the ball to the green without a second thought. To make extra sure you will hit the ball over the hazard, set up as normal but push your hands forward just a little more than usual.

Your weight should be about 65% on your left side. That way you are bound to hit down harder and firmer into the back of the ball. Hitting down gets the ball up. The only thing you need worry about is that you have sufficient club to get the ball the distance to the green.

For this it might help if you take one more club (a 7-iron rather than an 8) than you think you need and grip down a little more for greater control. Water always tends to shorten distances; and secondly that you have aligned the club face correctly.

The same goes every time you really feel you have to get the ball onto the putting surface. By taking extra club and gripping down very slightly you will increase your chance of getting the ball safely on the green. You should also be looking very carefully at the target to see where your safety zone is. If the green is long and narrow, for example, you risk missing it. Which side is it best to be on if you do miss it? Are there bunkers on one side that look very deep and difficult to get out of? If the green is on a plateau which side would

Playing over water or bunkers is no more difficult than playing over grass

For more control on any shot, grip down the club a little more, taking extra club if you need it. Never be short

Set up with about 65% of your weight towards your left side, take enough club and grip down slightly for extra control.

Hit down hard but don't try to do anything other than play your normal shot. Ignore the water. The camera crew here bet me a pint I couldn't hit eight balls across the lake without losing one. I needed the drink after that!

be the least difficult from which to play your next shot? If the green is an odd shape and the pin is cut on a narrow part, go for the "fat" of the green, giving yourself a better chance. Look for the safety zone on every shot — it always exists. Remember that you are looking to be able to play safe shots nine times out of ten, not once in a lifetime.

The worst shot you ever hit is the one where, the moment it goes wrong, you say to yourself, "I knew that wouldn't work". If you are driving your car and are faced with getting through a narrow gap you wouldn't try it if you seriously doubted you could squeeze through. You would find an alternative route. Why do anything different in golf? If you don't think you can get the ball where you want, you won't.

Try to avoid the negative thoughts that so often creep into golf. If you do miss the green, so what? Will it be the end of the world? Put it into perspective.

Later in this course I shall deal with the various short-shot situations you will encounter in golf from time to time; chipping over bunkers, hitting from the semi-rough around the green and looking to get the ball close to the pin when it is safe to do so.

For now, I urge you to practise your short game; always ensure you have enough club; and then play gentle shots to the heart of the green or to the side of the green where there is less trouble. Don't make life difficult.

Always aim for the "fat" of the green, rather than aiming directly at the pin

Practise the short game as often as you can if you really want to bring your scores down

Don't always go for the pin, aiming for the heart of the green if that is the safest shot, as here on a par-3 shot of 130 yards.

How to Love Bunkers

The average golfer hates bunkers. Professionals love them, preferring to be able to hit from the sand than from areas of semi-rough around the green. They know that from sand they can control the ball better. I am going to teach you to love bunkers.

Bunker shots are really quite simple and should present no problem to any golfer. Part of the difficulty, I suspect, is that if you do hit the ball into a greenside bunker, you are so disappointed at having missed the green that you are giving yourself negative thoughts. Until you have mastered bunker technique you will also be approaching the bunker with some trepidation, thus doubling your negativism.

Yet if you have played a shot towards the green from, say, 140 yards and it has gone into a greenside bunker, you have only missed the green by a few yards at most. From that distance it really is not that bad a result.

If you caught the bunker at least you managed to hit the ball virtually the correct distance!

Because the consistency of sand varies from course to course, and is affected by the amount of rain the course has sustained recently, you are likely to be faced with several different types of lies in bunkers. The worst is probably a plugged ball, but even then you can get it out safely though not necessarily into the best position for a single putt to save par. There are also

Laura Davies, Britain's top woman golfer, shows how easy it is to get out of sand first time, every time.

sloping lies which can be difficult to play from. We shall deal with those in our second section on more advanced golf.

For now we shall assume we have a reasonable lie in a fairly flat part of the bunker, that its face is not too steep and that there is a reasonable amount of green to work with. In these circumstances you will get the ball out first time, every time, and will be able to get the ball fairly close to the pin with a little practise.

During a round of golf you are not allowed to ground the club in the sand before you play the shot, not even on the take-away. In the practice bunker I am going to suggest that you do make some marks in the sand to help you.

Most bunker shots are fairly short so we use the shortest and most lofted club in the bag — the sand wedge. Unlike the other clubs it has a wide flange which is lower than the leading edge. Hold up a sand wedge and an ordinary wedge and you will see the difference.

The sand wedge was designed by Gene Sarazen, the great American golfer who won the 1922 US Open at the age of 20, going on to win the US PGA later that year, and again the following year. He also won both the British and US Opens in 1932 and the US Masters in 1935. It was after that last major victory that he decided the irons he and all the other golfers were using for sand were not quite good enough, so he set about designing a club that, instead of digging into the sand, as a normal club does, would bounce through the sand and splash the ball out softly.

One of the biggest problems in bunker play is psychological — you think that bunker shots are difficult, yet professionals would rather be in a bunker than just outside it

You must remember that you hit the sand, not the ball; the ball comes out on a cushion of sand

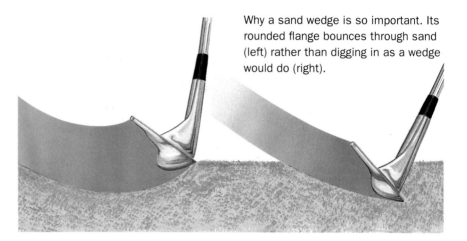

Why a sand wedge is so important. Its rounded flange bounces through sand (left) rather than digging in as a wedge would do (right).

As always you must align the club face at the target — the ball goes where you aim it

The closer you are to the pin, the more open you stand

Again, you have that straight line from your left shoulder to the club head

The flange on the modern sand wedge does just that, making it the best tool to use if you are in sand. What you then have to realise is that you do not hit the ball but the sand an inch or two behind it. As the club bounces through the sand it gets underneath the ball and lifts it out on a cushion of sand. If no sand comes out, no ball comes out.

In sand we do not want to hit the ball but the sand behind it, so the ball should be central in our stance.

Remember what I said earlier about the ball position appearing to alter as you altered your feet alignment. Set up square with the ball fairly central in your stance, then turn so that you are standing open to the target — in this case the flag. The ball will now appear to be further back in your stance and if you look at it from the point of view of the ball-to-target line it will be between the middle and back of your stance.

You must align the club face directly at the target, not right of it as some golf books incorrectly suggest. The ball goes where you aim it. If you want it to go right of the pin aim it to the right; if you want it to go at the pin, aim it at the pin. One of the reasons for the misunderstanding is that many people refer to holding the club "open". What they mean is open to the body target line, not to the real target. Always aim the club at your target.

You can shuffle your feet down in a bunker to help you keep a better balance in the sand as the last thing you want to do is slide around as you make the shot. It also helps to remind you that this, like all short shots, is more of an arm swing rather than one involving the lower body. Your feet will only move in the follow-through.

With the ball where it is your hands will be pressed slightly ahead of the ball, giving a slight, automatic wrist hinge. This helps you to get the club up slightly steeper than normal.

With your hands ahead of the ball you will also have automatically put about 65% of your weight onto your left side, which helps to get the club

For a straightforward bunker shot have the ball in the centre of your stance as you stand square, then turn to an open stance. Your weight is more towards your left side, a straight line from your left shoulder to the club head.

coming down into the sand behind the ball. Do make sure, though, that your head is behind the ball. It stays there throughout this, and every other, shot.

Keeping your head still, swing the club up fairly high, at least three-quarters length. You must swing slowly, not trying to rush it. You must also swing along your body line, not the ball-to-target line. When you are standing open the body line is aiming left of the target and you will swing along that line.

That helps to bring the club face across the ball from right to left, spinning the ball as it hits under it. That is what gets the ball up in the air, and also what will stop it when it lands, which is exactly what you want. The steeper you want the

Keep your head behind the ball throughout the shot

As you hit through the sand the club face is moving from right to left across the ball, helping to lift it out softly. Do follow through, not quitting on the shot.

Take a good three-quarters swing if you want to get the ball out. But remember to swing slowly and smoothly.

You must swing along your body line, not the ball-to-target line. That means you will be cutting across the ball from right to left, lifting it out with cut spin and making it stop quickly

You must hit fairly hard to get the ball out of a bunker; you could practise using an air ball; that will make you hit harder

To get the ball higher, stand more open but still aim the club face at the target

The higher the ball goes the "softer" it will land

ball to rise, and the quicker you want it to stop, the more open you stand to the target. It really is that easy to adjust the length you hit a bunker shot.

A bunker shot is the same as any other short shot, the only exception being that you aim to hit behind the ball.

I have said that you should swing to at least three-quarters length. That may cause you some concern if you only have fifteen yards between you and the pin. There is often the fear of over-hitting a shot out of sand but if you hit behind the ball as I have suggested you will never over-hit the ball. If you catch the ball first, thinning it, that is a different matter.

The main cause of thinning the ball from a bunker is that the player has raised his body on the back swing, thus ruining any chance of getting back into the address position at impact; or has tried to scoop the ball up in the air, causing him to fall back as the club approaches impact. That makes the club hit the ball, not the sand.

Keep your knees flexed and avoid any temptation to lift your head as you swing back. Also avoid the temptation of trying to scoop the ball up to get it out high; again that only results in a thinned shot, or worse.

As the flange of the sand wedge bounces through the sand it will lift the ball out and throw it high. As it comes down it should, because of its trajectory, land "softly" — not running much but staying almost where it lands. You can thus afford to hit it fairly hard. Try it in the practice bunker if your course has one. As long as you hit into the sand behind the ball, you can almost hit it as hard as you can

and the ball will still stop on the green. This is only valid if the sand is dry and soft — if it has been raining hard it could be a different matter because the sand will be compacted and the sand wedge will not bounce under the ball but above it. Playing from wet sand is a subject I shall deal with in the second part of our course.

You must make sure you follow through to a full, high finish; never quit on the shot; never leave the club in the sand or you will have decelerated the club as it approaches impact. If you leave the club in the sand you will leave the ball in the sand.

To help you when practising, I suggest you draw a few lines in the sand as I have done in the photograph. I have first of all shown the line from the ball to the target, then the feet line and finally the ideal ball position in that open stance.

I also practise by just hitting at sand. Having drawn two lines about six inches apart aim to hit the club into the sand on the first line and have it come out by the second line. This shows that you are hitting through the sand and not quitting on the shot.

The vast majority of golfers who leave the ball in the sand on the first attempt do so because they do not hit through the ball hard enough.

Try practising with one of those air balls. They are very light and you need to hit the sand smoothly and follow through to a high finish if you are to get the ball out. It really is very easy.

There are occasions when you need to cut off the follow through to stop the ball quickly but I shall deal with that later. For now concentrate on hitting to the fat part of the green and getting the ball out first time, every time. It will do wonders for your confidence.

Before we leave basic bunker technique, there are two situations you may well encounter and I will show you how to deal with them. The first is the plugged ball, where you might only be able to see the top half of the ball, if that; the second is where the ball is in a fairway bunker.

Plugged Ball
A plugged ball is not normally too bad for it does show that the sand is not rock hard. In fact it often means that the sand is light and powdery, so you can hit as hard as you like. You do, though, have to hit down more into the back of the

For a plugged ball you need to be well balanced, take a three-quarter swing and hit hard into the back of the ball.

Follow through if you want the ball to come out first time. Just flapping at the ball will leave it in the sand and you have wasted a shot

With a plugged ball you must stand rather more square, but remember, the ball will not stop quickly from this lie, but will run on, so aim for a part of the green where that shot will be safe

Because fairway bunkers tend to be flatter, you should have no problem hitting something like a 7-iron. Try to take it off the sand fairly cleanly, with very little divot

ball as you would for a normal shot off the fairway. Align yourself rather more square to the target with the club face square as well, the ball a little further back in your stance than midway, your hands ahead of the ball at address.

Take a three-quarter swing and hit slowly but smoothly. This can take some courage but it will get the ball out. Make sure you follow through to a full, high finish. Never quit on the ball when it is in a bunker.

Because you hit down on the ball when it is plugged you might find it easier to use a pitching wedge. With its sharp leading edge and no flange it will not bounce but will dig straight down into the sand. The club face hitting down into the back of the ball will lift it out safely, though you will not be able to control the ball once it lands. In these situations you might find it best to play to a safe area as I described a little earlier, instead of attempting to play straight at the flag, unless you have a lot of green to work with.

Fairway Bunkers
The other situation where you might find yourself in a bunker is out on the fairway. Fairway bunkers tend to be flatter than those guarding the greens, with no steep faces to hit over.

It is rare that you will be able to reach the green from a fairway bunker so your only safe option — and this is what golf is all about — is to play the ball to an area of safety.

Take something like a 7-iron, align square to your target — having chosen the spot from where you would ideally like to play your next shot — grip down the club a

little and play the ball in the middle of your stance. Settle your feet securely but don't shuffle down too much or you will risk hitting the sand behind the ball. It helps your balance if you stand slightly knock-kneed.

In a fairway bunker you need to take the ball cleanly off the sand, the club hitting the ball first and not taking any sand. You could almost thin the ball and get it out.

You may find at first that you are taking too much sand so the ball will not go as far as you would like from a fairway bunker. You must resist the temptation to hit extra hard as this will just throw you off balance and result in an even worse shot. You are better hitting a shorter iron because the swing arc is narrower than for a 4-iron, for example. Remember, though, swing slowly and try to sweep the club through the impact zone rather than hitting down on the ball as you do on a fairway. It is a different shot and will take you some time to master, but you must persevere with it.

If you have a good distance to go — over about 150 yards to the green — I am going to suggest you hit the easiest shot you could. This is, however, only if you have a bunker with no high lip in front of you. In such a situation I would hit a 5-wood, and for two main reasons. Firstly, it will hit the ball high enough and long enough. Secondly, it will not dig into the sand but will take the ball off the surface cleanly, which is exactly what you want.

I have seen professionals hit the driver from a flat fairway bunker but that's taking things a bit far.

If you have a high lip to the bunker or are close to the front

You will find that the club digs into the sand more so you will not get such a high follow-through, though never try to quit — do hit hard through impact.

edge, this option might not be open to you. In that case get out of the bunker with the minimum effort, first time. The motto in golf is — keep it simple.

If you practise these routines and follow the procedure I have outlined in this chapter you will never fear bunkers again, because as you approach one you will know that you will get the ball out first time, every time.

Finally, as we are leaving the sand, please do remember to rake

the bunker. If there is no rake try to smooth the surface with your feet rather than your club.

A continuing debate questions where you should leave the rake after you have finished with it — in the bunker or on the grass near it? You should leave it in the bunker, preferably as far away from the normal line of flight towards the green. If you leave it outside the bunker a ball could hit it and be diverted into the bunker. If the rake is in the bunker that will not happen and, should the ball lodge under the rake, you are allowed to move the rake without penalty, even if you dislodge the ball. Rakes belong in bunkers.

If in doubt, get it out. A simple motto but one worth remembering if you have a difficult lie or the bunker face is steep. You can play sideways or even backwards, but get the ball out first time

Above left With 150 yards or so to go from a fairway bunker, take something like a 7-iron and adopt a fairly square stance. Only take a three-quarter back swing as you must maintain your balance.

Above Your aim is to take the ball off the surface cleanly, with little sand.

Left Although you want to avoid too much body movement on the shot you should end up by facing the target, as with a normal shot of this length.

Right For a longer shot, and with a fairly flat bunker, I would hit a 5-wood, though you must be a fairly competent player to attempt this. The ball is swept off the surface fairly cleanly, though never try to over-hit it.

A Rough Time

Most golfers end up in the rough from time to time — some more often than others! When I first started playing I seemed to spend more time in the deep grass than on the fairway.

Even top tournament professionals veer off the fairway regularly as you can see at any tournament, so it really is nothing to be ashamed of. Nor is it something you should let get the better of you.

What I am going to do is to show you how to get the ball out of the rough first time, every time, just as we did from the bunker. In fact, bunker shots and recovery shots from deep rough are very similar.

The first thing to do is to go in and find the ball, of course, which is sometimes not easy, particularly if you play on some of the courses I do, where players have been known to go in looking for a ball and have never been seen again! Links courses are often better, unless you get in among the heather and gorse.

As with a shot which has dived into a bunker you must put out of your mind any negative thoughts, even though you probably have more justification in being somewhat annoyed about finding the rough than you should ending up in a bunker. Negative thoughts lead to negative actions.

Concentrate your mind fully on getting the ball out. You have hit a bad shot to go into the rough. Now work on hitting a good shot to get out.

I am going to deal first with very deep rough, the sort that comes up

well over your ankles and probably higher than that. There will be times when the ball is so deep in the rough that you really have little chance of hitting it. You always have the option of minimising your losses by declaring the ball unplayable, swallowing the medicine of a penalty stroke and dropping the ball in a more friendly position. This is an extreme case and I hope it is only a sensible option in very rare circumstances, but if it is the only **sensible** option then you must give it very careful consideration. As I have mentioned before golf is about playing sensibly.

The first thing you should do is to find a suitable place on the fairway where you want to land the ball. Far too many golfers just go into the rough and try to hit the ball as hard as possible, without any real target. As we have seen earlier, on every shot you need a definable target or target area.

Walk out onto the fairway and see which position would be a good one from which to take your **next** shot. Always think ahead. Be realistic about it, not marching forward 200 yards if you have little realistic chance of hitting the ball more than 50 yards. Make sure that, from where your ball is in the rough, you have a clear shot to this target. If it involves hitting the ball

---

Even the world's top players stray into the rough now and again. Their first concern, every time, is to get out to a safe position. Their range of options is possibly greater than yours and mine, but follow their example and get out of the rough safely first time.

Be realistic when you are in the rough; your sole aim is the get the ball back onto short grass in one shot

---

When you are in the rough take the time to walk out onto the fairway and see where you should be aiming if you want to take your next shot from the ideal position

Left Check carefully that no overhanging branches will interfere with your back swing.

Right In deep rough your sand wedge could be your best friend. Stand fairly open as the club head will snag as you hit through.

Below As you set up your weight will favour your left side; keep it there throughout the swing.

It is a good idea to take a few practice swings in the rough; that way you will see just how strong the grass is and how much it will hinder the club head

Long grass will snag the club, turning it closed. To compensate, aim a little right

Hit hard, but follow through if you want the ball to come out

out through trees, look carefully for low-hanging branches or anything else that might snag the ball or interfere with your back swing. Remember, your only aim is to get the ball safely back on the fairway.

Sometimes this might mean hitting out sideways or even back towards the tee, but if either of those is the only safe option, then do it. Don't waste shots.

If you do have overhanging branches on your safest route you might have to keep the ball low, but if it is in deep rough that might be very difficult. As I said, don't discount declaring it unplayable — you should never take two shots to get out of the rough.

Having chosen your target and

your route, you may find that your sand wedge is your best friend, partly because it is the shortest club in the bag. With any over-hanging branches likely to interfere with your swing that is a factor worth considering.

Your set up and aim are as important here as anywhere else on the course. On almost every other shot you aim the club face directly at where you want the ball to go. In deep rough the grass will snag the club and will catch it first on the hosel, where the club and shaft meet. This will pull the club

Hit down hard, your hands pulling on the club to promote a sharp downward blow into the grass behind the ball, in a very similar fashion to a bunker shot.

face closed at impact so allow a little for this, just as we shall do later in this series of lessons when we deal with sloping lies.

This means aiming very slightly to the right of your target, though not too much. Still stand square with the ball fairly well back in your stance to promote a steep, downward strike into the back of the ball. Your weight should be pushed fairly well towards the target, about 65% or so on your left foot. That sets your hands nicely ahead of the ball, recreating the almost straight line from the left shoulder to the club head that we had on short shots much earlier.

I would suggest a couple of practice swings first. This will give you an idea of how hard you will have to hit to get the club through the grass.

When you are ready, having chosen your target and your route, swing the club back up fairly fully and hit down as hard as you can whilst still retaining control of the club head. Pick the club up fairly steeply; with the way you are standing, the ball further back in your stance than normal, your hands will already be slightly hinged. It is that which will help you take the club away more steeply than usual.

As you swing down into the ball have the feeling that you are

Hit right through the ball, keeping the club head going or you risk leaving the club — and the ball — in the rough.

moving ahead of the ball, pulling the club head through the ball. You do need to hit hard, even if you do not have too far to go. Again, think of how we had to hit hard to get out of the bunker. This really is very similar.

The follow-through is still an important part of the shot, for it demonstrates that you have hit through the ball. Of course the long grass might slow down the club head and you might not have too much room to make a full follow-through, but you must not quit on the shot or you risk leaving the ball in the long grass.

Lighter Rough
Thankfully, not all rough is waist high and just off the edges of most fairways you will encounter an area of light rough. This presents a completely different opportunity

for now you have the possibility of hitting the ball a very long way.

Again, though, your first decision is to choose a realistic target. Because you are off the fairway it is possible that your route to the green may be blocked by a tree. In this case you have to take the easy option, hitting the ball to a safe spot on the fairway, just as before.

Look very carefully at the way the grass has been cut. If it is growing more towards you the shot will need to be firmer and you may need to allow for the club face closing as it hits into the grass. You will need to aim slightly right of your intended target in that case. You might also need to use a stronger club than you would use for the distance, say a 7-iron instead of an 8.

If the grass is growing towards

Light rough can cause problems as you often think the shot will be easy; learn to understand the pitfalls though, and practise playing from rough sometimes to understand what happens to the ball

When the ball is sitting up, be very careful that you do not slide the club under it as that will hit it higher, but less distance.

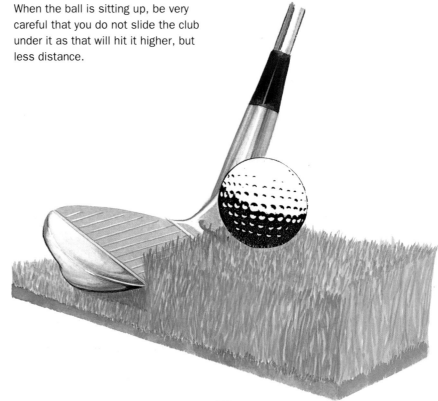

the hole you will have an easier shot but may get what is known as a "flyer", the ball not stopping when it lands. In this case take one less club (a 9-iron instead of an 8, for instance), and you could hit with slightly more of an open stance.

Another thing to look at very carefully is the lie of the ball. It might be sitting up high on the grass, or it might be sitting down, half-hidden. In some ways the second is better, because it will force you to hit hard and down into the ball. If it is sitting up too much you risk sliding the club under the ball, effectively skying it with a consequent lack of distance.

If it is sitting down, your set up will depend mainly on the shot you are trying to play. If it is short, just to get the ball out onto the fairway maybe about 100 yards or so, play it just like a normal short shot from the fairway, but as if you were trying to hit over a bunker. Have the ball a little back in your stance, setting your hands ahead of the ball, a good, straight line from your left shoulder down through your left arm and shaft to the club head.

Aim the club face at your target; if the grass snags the hosel it will only do so slightly so you should not need to make any allowance for this, unless the grass is wet or, as you take a couple of practice swings, you notice the club head is really getting caught up. If that is the case aim slightly to the right of where you want the ball to finish.

Have your weight about 65% to your left side and be very careful to keep it there during the swing, rather than moving too far on the back swing. Only swing about three-quarters at most or you risk losing your balance. As with all other short shots, accelerate the club through the ball fairly hard, not slowing down but hitting through to a good finish.

If the ball is sitting up, which often happens when the grass is growing in spring and early summer, or if you are playing on one of the strong grasses, like Bermuda grass in the United States or couch in Australia, your choice of shot depends very much on what you are trying to achieve.

If you have a short shot of, say, 100 yards to the green, it is very similar to any other shot of that distance, but beware, as you risk sliding the club too much under the ball. You must keep in mind that the club will always find the lowest point it can. Thus, on a normal fairway shot you take a divot as the club reaches lower than the bottom of the ball. It will do the same here, so if the grass is an inch high the club will hit an inch below the ball rather than down into the back of it as it should. That hits it higher but reduces its distance. Very often you will need to take one or two clubs more than you think for the same distance, particularly if you have a bunker or something to carry to reach the green.

Stand with the ball about the centre of your stance; your feet and shoulder line could be very, very slightly open, though I prefer a square stance for this shot. Your weight again is about 65% on your left foot. Try to keep it there as much as possible throughout the swing, though as you will be swinging fairly fully it will not be totally possible to remain still. Feel natural, just concentrating on swinging the club up and down

Coming out of light rough the ball may take a "flyer", not stopping once it hits the green; you may want to allow for this in your choice of club

When the ball is sitting up you may slide the club under the ball, hitting it higher but shorter; take enough club

The 3-wood from light rough — one of the best shots you can get. Treat it just as you would a tee shot, with a full swing and a hard drive through the ball as the weight transfers to your left, bringing your body round to face the target at the finish. You ought to be able to hit this as far as any drive.

With a long shot from light rough use the 3-wood and treat it just like a tee shot, though it may fade very slightly so allow for this

As this shot will run more on landing, ensure you have your target correct

and let the rest of the body react naturally. As always keep one eye focused on the ball so that you try to keep your head fairly still.

Hit through fully and don't try to stop the club.

Finally, we have what many golfers think is the best shot they can find — the ball sitting up perfectly in the semi-rough and 240 yards to the green. This is where the 3-wood comes in handy. You could even use the driver, particularly if you have a slight left-to-right dog-leg.

Treat this just as you would a shot using a tee-peg. Set up with the ball slightly forward in your stance, just inside the left instep. As you place the club head behind the ball it should nestle down into the grass so the top of the club will be about level with the equator of the ball — just as on a tee shot.

Take the club away smoothly and swing just as you would with any long club. I know this is an area we have not yet reached but as we shall be coming to it soon, in the second series of lessons, all you need to know is that you swing smoothly and slowly. The ball will come out easily and fly well to the target.

One tiny word of warning, though. A ball hit like this will not stop suddenly on landing, but will run for some distance, particularly on a hard fairway, so be careful that you don't over-hit it.

We shall deal with delicate shots out of rough around the green a little later as they are rather specialist type shots.

Get out of that! Nick Faldo proves his skills by recovering from a difficult situation at Valderrama in the 1992 Volvo Masters.

Sink that Putt!

Putting is the one vital part of golf for it is the only time you get the ball in the hole — unless you are good enough to be able to score a hole-in-one off the tee or chip the ball straight in from off the green. These rarities apart, you need to be able to putt.

More shots are wasted on the greens than anywhere else on the golf course. The par of the average course is 72; that should include 36 putts — half your score. Next time you play a round of golf, count the number of putts you take — make a little extra note on your scorecard. If you take less than 36 you are doing all right. Any more than 40 and you are in urgent need of help. Top professionals get round in under 30!

Very few people practise their putting sufficiently. If they did the putting greens would be as busy as the driving ranges. And have you ever heard of anyone taking a putting lesson?

A number of players believe that, as putting involves very little movement, it is not a skill that can be acquired and honed, as can bunker play or driving, for example. They are wrong. Putting requires skill and judgement, as do driving, chipping and every other aspect of golf. If a round of golf should involve 50% of your shots being putts, you ought to spend half your time practising putting. Very few people, with the exception of top tour players, spend that much time on the putting green.

The first thing to get right about putting is to buy the correct putter. This may sound obvious but you would be amazed at the number of golfers who do not have a putter which suits them.

Not all golfers are the same height and although clubs generally come in fairly standard lengths, putters do vary. Apart from those extra long ones — the so-called broom-handle putters — used by some professionals like Sam Torrance and Peter Senior, putters vary in length. Women's putters are often an inch or so shorter.

It would seem pretty stupid for a 6'4" player to have the same length putter as someone of only 5'4" but this invariably happens. I know the taller player has longer arms but even so, a longer handled putter would surely be more beneficial to the taller player.

Your first priority, then, is to buy a putter with which you are comfortable. Fortunately you can try putters out first, either on the putting green or on an artificial putting surface at a golf shop. My advice is to try several until you get the one you feel happy with. Try various lengths, and various head shapes. They vary in shape considerably and some of them seem to be designed more by modern sculptors than golfers. Many are heavier than others, which can be beneficial on slow greens but on a lightning fast surface a heavy putter could over-hit the ball. However, it

Payne Stewart, the popular American golfer, sends another putt rolling smoothly to the hole. The professionals spend far more time lining up their putts, taking more care on the greens than amateur players. Perhaps this is why they hole so many!

More shots are wasted on the putting green than anywhere else on the golf course: on average professionals take around 29 putts per round; how many do you take?

Although putting accounts for half the score in a round of golf, very few people spend half their time practising their putting skills comes down to personal choice and, most importantly, effectiveness.

Putting styles vary almost as much as putters. Some people stand very upright; others are bent over almost double. Some have a fairly normal putting grip whilst others grip the club in a most unorthodox fashion. Even among the professional ranks styles vary considerably.

In this section, though, we are going to look at one basic method of putting — the one which the majority of teaching professionals the world over use with their pupils. Learn this one first. If it does not work for you then it might be time to try a few variations in stance and grip. More advanced putting techniques follow later in this course, but master the basics first.

First, as with all our shots,

· comes the pre-shot routine, including the decision as to the length of the shot and the alignment of the putter. You also have to work out the slope of the green and to decide whether it is fast or slow. An uphill putt needs to be hit harder than one going downhill. A wet green slows the ball down more so you need to hit it harder.

Assume for this exercise that the green is perfectly flat, so we have no borrow to worry about. Very few golfers know the length of the putt facing them and whilst not suggesting that you pace out each one, on a very long putt it can be of benefit to walk to the pin and back, particularly for an uphill putt.

Having decided how hard the ball needs to be struck, the next thing to do is to align the putter head. You often see professionals these days lining the putter up in front of the ball and if it helps you then do it. The majority of players line up behind the ball.

Most putters these days have a white mark on the top of the putter head denoting the centre of the club and acting as an aid to correct alignment. Use these as much as you can, making sure the line points to the hole. As with other shots you can stand behind the ball to make sure of your line, though you cannot putt croquet-style.

Use the white mark on the top of the putter to help with your alignment.

An uphill putt needs to be hit firmly, more so than on a flat green. Obvious, but many golfers seem to forget.

Take the time to walk from the ball to the pin, looking carefully at the length, the slope of the green and to repair any pitch marks

Most putters have a white line or mark on them to help you with your alignment

Once you have the line, take your stance. Most golfers find it comfortable to have their feet fairly close together for a putt, but this is really a matter of personal choice. Don't have your feet too wide apart or it might cause you to sway. One exception is if you are putting in very strong wind. In those circumstances you may find you are better balanced with your feet slightly wider apart.

The feet alignment for a putt is normally slightly open. This will allow your arms to swing through unhindered as you strike the ball. In the full swing the hips turn left out of the way, allowing space for the arms to swing the club down and through. As there is virtually no body movement in the putting stroke, we need to create this space from the beginning.

However, the shoulders at address should be square to the target. Your weight should be very slightly towards your left foot, as you are slightly leaning towards the target.

Ball position is important. Ideally it should be a little forward in your stance. Your hands should be very slightly ahead of the ball, so that the putter shaft is leaning slightly towards the target. Once again there ought to be a fairly straight line from your left shoulder to the putter head.

Don't overdo this or you will not be able to strike the ball correctly. You do, however, need to have your eyes directly over the

Keep your feet fairly close together when you putt as that will help you to use your shoulders more in the swing

Although you stand with your feet slightly open you must keep your shoulders parallel to the target line as that is where you will then swing

You will find it helpful to stand with your feet slightly open for a putt, but try to keep your shoulders fairly square. I find it best to stand tall to a putt, rather than stooping over as some golfers do.

Your feet should not be too wide and the ball is towards the front of your stance.

ball, so if it is too far forward you will have a problem. Some players try to have their weight evenly distributed and the ball central in their stance but I feel this can often cause a putt which is off to the right, so I suggest you play it a little forward of centre. That in turn will cause you to lean your weight slightly toward the hole to get your eyes directly over the ball.

One more tiny word about the stance at this point. You will have seen many players stoop right over when putting. Bernhard Langer is one; Jack Nicklaus another. To be honest the taller you can stand to a putt the more chance you have of holing it. Both these fine golfers have suffered terribly on the putting greens during their careers though they have used different techniques to cure their problems. Forget problems — do it right.

Try not to bend over too much as it can affect the movement of the arms and cause you to miss putts. The important thing is to have your eyes directly above the ball. To check this get yourself into position and ready to putt, then hold another ball on the bridge of your nose and let it drop. If it hits the ball on the ground you are in the correct position.

You could also hold the putter with the grip on the bridge of your nose. If the putter head obliterates the ball, again, you are in the correct position. Check it, and check it regularly.

The most popularly used grip is the reverse overlap, which, as the name implies, is a reversal of the Vardon grip used for most other shots. It entails gripping the club in the normal way, then releasing the little finger of the right hand and the index finger of the left, and

Check that your eyes are directly above the ball by holding a putter between your eyes. It should cover the ball.

Although some players stoop right over their putts it is probably better if you stand tall to the putt

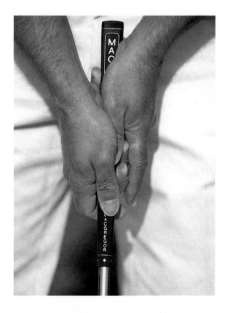

The most widely used putting grip is a reverse overlap, the little finger of the right hand and the index finger of the left changing places.

Your eyes should be above the ball; to check this drop a ball from the bridge of your nose; it should hit the ball on the ground

The putter head should finish aiming at the target on all putts, long or short

Try to rock your shoulders up and down like a pendulum rather than turning them

To get the ball rolling straighter, hit it slightly on the upswing, the putter head catching it on its equator

reversing their position, so that the little finger of the right hand is firmly on the club. The left index finger is then held fairly straight rather than curling round the grip. Holding it straight has a benefit which we shall come to shortly, though you can curl it round the right hand a little.

Now for the putt itself. There are two basic putting strokes, the "push" and the "tap". Some top tour players, like Fred Couples, tend to tap the ball, using a short back swing and a quick stab at the ball before stopping the putter head. This does, however, create many potential problems and I strongly recommend that you keep to the more widely used "push" putt.

In its simplest terms this means that the putter head is swung back and through at a standard pace, not decelerating as it impacts with the ball. The proof of a correctly swung putter is if the putter head finishes pointing at the target.

At address we have set the hands on the club in such a way that, when looked at from the front, your arms and the putter shaft would form a large "Y". The aim in putting is to maintain the shape of this "Y" throughout the stroke.

If you think about this it will become apparent that to maintain that shape your wrists will remain firm, not bending or cocking as they do in a full swing.

One way to get the feeling for this movement is to stand with your palms together in front of you, but without a putter. Just swing your arms gently back and forward, keeping the palms together, but making sure you do not bend your wrists.

If you keep your head still and

just let your shoulders rock up and down — like a pendulum — you will understand what is required in the putting stroke.

When you then hold the putter and use the same pendulum motion, keeping your wrists firm, you will hole more putts. You should keep in mind the follow-through which, as we have seen earlier, is important in golf, even though it is something that happens after you have hit the ball.

On a putt the club goes back 45% and through 55% — yet again. By keeping the wrists firm — as we did on the short shot with the 7-iron much earlier — we finish with the left arm and club shaft forming a straight line. It must be the same on putts. Extend your arms through the ball, aiming the putter head at a second target just ahead of you. You should finish with the "Y" still in place and the putter head aimed directly at the target. This is particularly important on a very short putt of just a foot or so, when you should finish with the putter head over the hole itself. That will ensure the ball is on the right track for the hole.

Earlier in this course of lessons we saw how the ball will always spin when it is hit. It is the spin that gets it airborne. On the green the ball does not spin — it rolls. It cannot be hit with backspin, topspin or sidespin. All you do is roll it. To get it to roll straight you will find it simpler to hit it on the equator, unlike a normal shot with an iron when you hit it with a descending blow.

Athough you address the ball with the putter on the ground, which helps you align the putter head correctly, you should be looking to strike the ball with the

To understand and feel the putting "swing" stand with your palms together and gently rock your shoulders from side to side, like a pendulum, the hands staying firm throughout.

With a putter the movement is the same. It is vital the hands stay firm.

putter head slightly off the ground. In effect the putter is then rising as it strikes the ball, helping to roll it in such a way that it stays on line better.

You also need to keep your head very still whilst putting. On a short putt the saying is that you should hear the ball drop rather than see it. Concentrate on looking at the back of the ball as you putt, but then keep looking at the same spot until well after the ball has begun its roll towards the hole.

The strength of the putt will obviously depend on the distance to the hole, the slope and the speed of the green, but again this is not really something you can learn from a book — you need to go and practise. On the next couple of pages you will find some practice routines that will help you improve your putting. The second section of this course also deals in more detail with advanced putting techniques that are essential to lowering your handicap.

Before we leave putting, though, a brief word about sloping greens. If the green slopes from left to

right between the ball and the hole, it should be fairly obvious that you need to aim the ball to the left of the hole, above it. The ball will follow gravity and the slope and, as it loses speed, will begin rolling to the right, down the slope. Judging the exact amount of "borrow" — the distance up the slope you need to hit the ball to get it to finish by or in the hole — takes time and patient practice. Much depends on the pace of the green and the angle of the slope.

Many professionals use plumb-bobbing to help them estimate the amount of borrow. I have detailed what they look for later, but it is not a foolproof method. Only time and experience will teach you, and you still need to read the pace of the greens. If only every green was flat! But then that would take some of the skill out of golf, wouldn't it?

Finally, please repair your pitch marks and any which less caring golfers have left on the greens. When a ball lands on the green, particularly if the ground is soft, an indentation mark remains. If left unrepaired for 15 minutes the ground will take at least three weeks to "heal". It can be repaired in seconds, if done immediately.

As the ball landed it did not push the surface downwards, but spread it outwards, just as dropping a stone in a pond causes ripples to flow outwards. To repair a pitch mark you need to push that displaced soil back towards the centre, rather than lifting it up from underneath.

As you do push it back in from the sides it will be raised slightly above the normal surface so tap it down gently with the putter head to leave a smooth surface.

> Your head must remain very still during a putt. You can practise by closing your eyes as soon as you hit the ball — it is then pointless looking up

> On a sloping green choose a midway point between the ball and hole and try to judge the line from there to the pin; then judge it from there to your ball

To stroke the ball straight you will find it helps to hit the ball on its equator.

Practising Your Putting Skills

1   Round the Clock

This is a good routine on a slightly sloping practice green. It involves placing twelve balls in a circle around the hole and then trying to hole each one. Any time you miss one go back to the beginning and start all over again until you can get all twelve balls in the hole three times running.

Start with the balls about two feet from the hole and, once you can hole every time three times, move back another foot and repeat the exercise.

You will find that twelve balls do not fit in one hole together so after you have six in the hole safely, pick them out. That makes you regrip and set up again properly.

2 One to Ten

This involves placing one golf ball about two feet from the hole and marking its position by a tee-peg. Hole it, then replace it, adding a second ball a further twelve inches back. Hole both balls, then replace them and add a third a further foot away and so on until you have ten balls at one foot intervals. Again you must hole every one of them. Any time you miss one start from the beginning again. By the time you have successfully holed six or seven you will begin to feel the emotional pressure you might feel on the course when faced with a crucial putt.

3   A Quick Nine
This is one I use when the practice putting green is fairly quiet and
normally at the end of a practice session. Many practice greens have
nine holes cut in them though if yours has less don't worry. It
doesn't really matter whether you play six or nine holes, though I
think six is the minimum.

Using three golf balls — use good ones for all your putting
practice routines, not old, scratched or scuffed ones — start from
any position and hole all three balls in two, that is two-putt each ball.
Try to vary the length of each hole and don't be afraid to choose
your own way round if your practice green has numbered holes.

For the three balls you should score six per hole, making a total of
54 for nine holes. The aim is to get round in "par". Think it's easy?
Try it.

How to Beat the Golf Course

Having learnt the art of playing some of the golf shots you are likely to need, the next thing to do is to get out on the golf course and beat your own personal par.

That introduces an interesting point, for the majority of players get to a tee and automatically think in terms of the par of the hole, either 3, 4 or 5.

Yet each golfer has a handicap, and each hole has a stroke index.

If you have a high handicap, above 18, you may well find one or more holes where you are allowed to take two shots over the nominal par, say a five on a par-3, and still achieve a net par.

The first thing you should do on the tee is to look at the stroke index of the hole and see how many shots you are allowed to take, using your handicap, to achieve a "par". The average golfer, playing off a handicap of around 16, will have an extra stroke on all but a couple of the holes on the course. My advice is to use them.

Even newcomers to golf should be looking not at the distance but how many shots they have to reach the green.

I will give you an example. On the 9th at La Manga, a par-5, the stroke index is 2. Anyone with a handicap higher than 2 – the vast majority of golfers – is thus allowed

to take six shots on that hole, four of them to reach the green and two putts.

Most players would, on reaching the tee and seeing that they have 577 yards to reach the green, would use the driver, hitting as hard as they possibly could. Over-hitting leads to loss of control which means loss of direction and the ball could end in the rough, or worse.

Yet they have four shots to cover 577 yards, making 144 yards per shot. Most players could hit that distance comfortably with a 6-iron. So why try to blast the driver out of sight?

At La Manga on the 9th (south course) I did just that, joined by two of the camera crew, to see whether it was possible to reach the green with four shots using a medium iron. Using just a 7-iron and hitting regular shots rather than trying to hit extra hard, two of us made the green in three, the other was 20 yards short on the third shot so made it comfortably in four.

It may not be very macho to use a 6-iron off the tee on a par-5 but if you want to play safe, and to your handicap, that would appear to be the sensible option, yet nobody takes it.

Next time you play, on your local course, choose one par-5 where you gain an extra shot, allowing you four to reach the green. Try it as I have just described it, hitting a 5-iron all the way, including off the tee. Four 5-irons will get you safely on the

Royal Portrush in Northern Ireland, one of the most frightening golf courses in strong wind. A wonderful challenge to any golfer and a marvellous golf course; in my opinion one of the best in the world.

green, though I would almost guarantee you will not need a 5-iron for your fourth shot as you will be closer to the green than you imagined. You will probably need no more than an 8-iron.

Why, then, do so many people struggle on long par-5 holes?

The answer is fear. Fear of being short; fear of appearing to lack the power to reach the green with a driver and two good shots. Yet the average golfer rarely has to reach the green of a par-5 in just three shots if he or she would only take advantage of their handicap.

Golf is a game of strategy, rather like chess. It favours the cunning, not the foolish.

On the following pages you will find a few examples of situations which regularly occur during a round of golf. I have mixed in a couple of matchplay situations to add some extra pressure, as you do need to consider what you would do if you either need to protect a lead or to attack your opponent from a couple of strokes or holes behind. Although matchplay is an excellent form of golf you should

also consider that, in strokeplay, you are not playing an opponent but the course itself. If you need to avoid dropping shots for your best round ever, then you are almost in a matchplay situation against the par of the course.

Always remember, though, that you can never save shots — you can only avoid wasting them.

In these partly hypothetical situations I have set the scene but not given you the answer, because that will depend on your ability and your level of confidence at the time.

There is, in fact, no definite answer for we would all look at the problem from a different point of view.

Go through them and decide what you would do. I would then suggest you discuss them with a friend to see what he or she would do in the same circumstances. You could also write to me with your solutions. I will send you back my suggestions and comments and tell you how I would play them. Good luck.

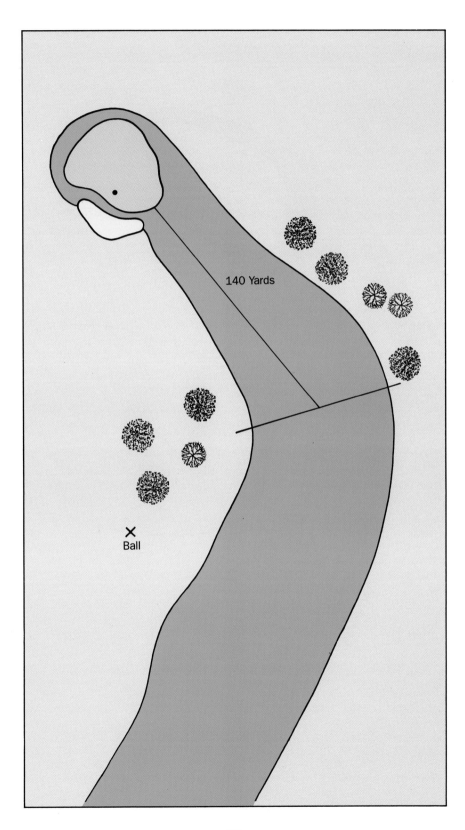

140 Yards

✕
Ball

The first situation is with the ball under some trees just off the fairway on a dog-leg. The distance from the corner of the dog-leg to the front of the green is 140 yards, so the ball is about 160 yards from the front of the green in a straight line. The right side of the fairway is tree-lined and there is a deep bunker off the right side of the green.

The ball is sitting up fairly well in fluffy grass so it would be possible to hit it cleanly. There are no overhanging branches to restrict your swing, though there is a tree directly on your line to the green.

In situation (a) you are all square with your opponent in a matchplay situation; this is the 15th hole and he has pushed his tee shot into the trees on the right. He has no direct shot at the green and will probably have to chip out and drop a shot.

In situation (b) you are a stroke down on him in strokeplay and his tee shot is in the centre of the fairway 155 yards from the front of the green.

In situation (c) you are one-up in matchplay and your opponent is in the centre of the fairway.

In this example you have 190 yards to the front of the green but the shot is across water. There is also a large bunker guarding the front right of the green. Your opponent has just hit his second shot into that bunker and will probably drop one shot.

In matchplay you are all-square and this is the 17th hole.

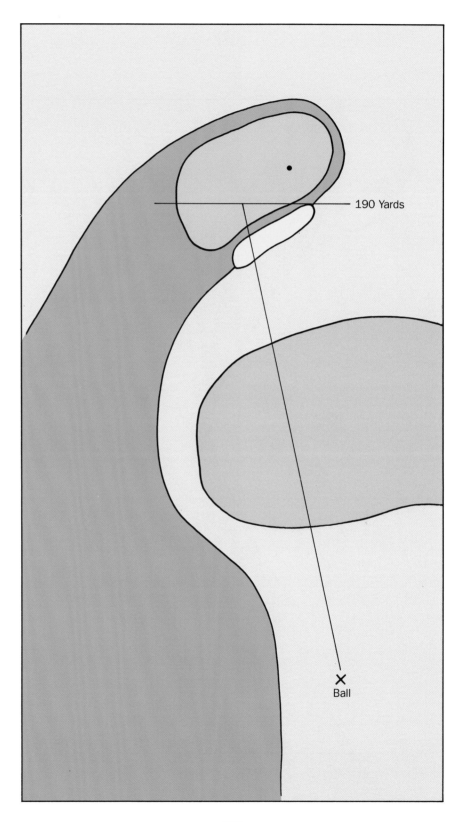

190 Yards

X
Ball

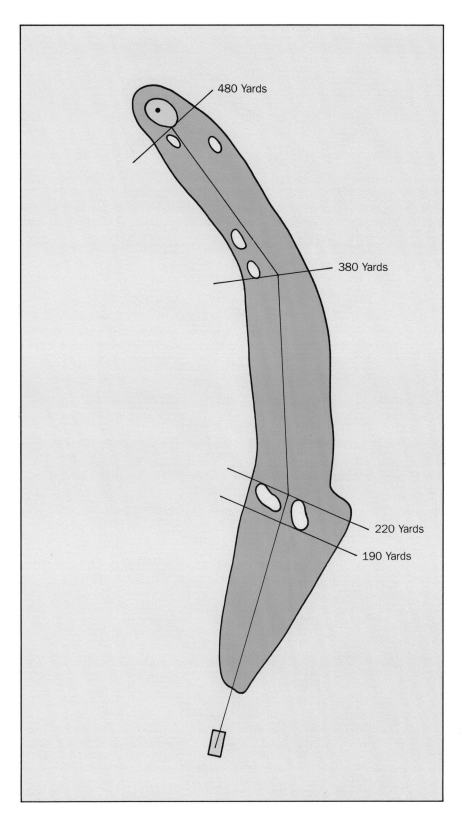

480 Yards

380 Yards

220 Yards

190 Yards

This is based on the par-5 12th hole at Kingston Heath GC, in Melbourne, Australia, though I have taken artistic licence and added something. The hole measures 485 yards with the distance from the tee to the fairway bunkers being 230 yards. Being a par-5 you could lay up short of the bunkers from the tee, though if you do that you have little chance of reaching the dog-leg with your second shot and will need four to reach the green.

In situation (a) your opponent has driven over the bunkers; he is two-up with six to play after this hole.

In situation (b) you have just won the last hole to go one-up.

In situation (c) you have just won the last hole to square the match and this is now the 18th.

This is another shot over water, though the distance to the front of the green is only 147 yards. The pin is cut a further 4 yards onto the green and the depth of the green as you look at it is 9 yards, so you don't have much room. There is a grass bank at the back of the green with fairly short grass. That should give you a clue.

Your opponent is on the green in two though has a long putt up and over a ridge, making it difficult for him to get close enough to guarantee his par.

In situation (a) you are all-square on the 15th hole.

In situation (b) you are one-up on the 15th hole.

In situation (c) you are four shots behind in strokeplay and this is the 13th hole.

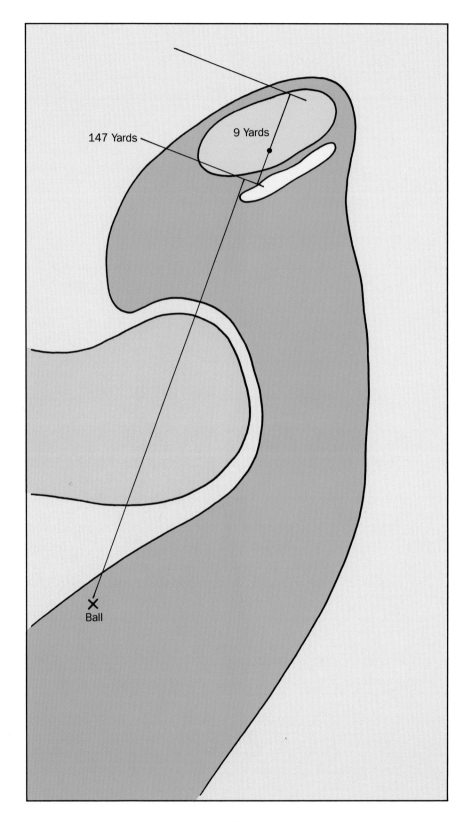

147 Yards

9 Yards

Ball

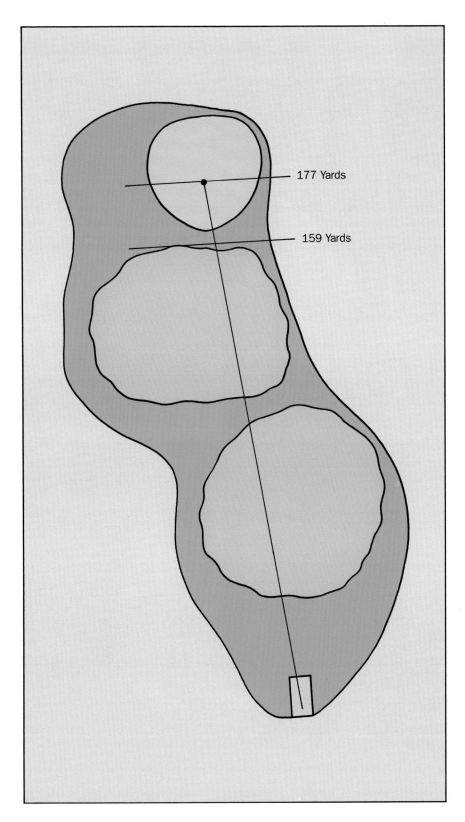

177 Yards

159 Yards

Finally, the 11th hole from Wörthsee, near Munich in Germany, and yet another hole with water. The hole measures 177 yards to the centre of the green; 159 yards to carry the water. You are hitting into a strong wind and it is raining hard.

In situation (a) you are three strokes behind your opponent in strokeplay, but he has just hit his tee shot into the lake.

In situation (b) you are one-down in matchplay and your opponent has just missed the green left, leaving him an awkward chip to the green.

In situation (c), in strokeplay, you are two-over but your opponent is three-over. You are to play first. He took four on both the previous two par-3s; you took a three and a four.

Power Driving

Everyone wants to be able to drive the ball 300 yards straight down the middle of the fairway. If you go to professional tournaments you will probably stand and gaze in awe as player after player launches missiles down the fairway amazing distances.

I have been fortunate enough to work with some of the longest hitters of a golf ball in the world over many years and it never ceases to amaze me how they can achieve such distance with so little apparent effort.

How do they do it? More to the point, how can *you* do it?

Let me show you.

Earlier in this course I dealt with the essential ingredients of a good golf swing, explaining how the swing should be smooth and, particularly on the back swing, fairly slow. There is no point rushing the back swing because at some point the club comes to a complete stop before it reverses direction.

The club only needs to pick up speed from the top of the back swing until it has passed through the impact zone. Note I never said "until it hits the ball". It must go through and "hit" a second "ball" a foot or so in front of the real ball.

If you can achieve this feeling on every shot, that you are playing a second "ball" as well, you will be well on the way to swinging a golf club correctly.

Another essential ingredient to produce power is that you turn

Greg Norman presents a portrait of power as another missile is launched almost 300 yards down the fairway.

your shoulders fully on the back swing. Really work hard on getting them as far round as you can, to at least 90° from their position at address, square to the target line.

To achieve extra power the more experienced golfer can "cheat" a little by standing very slightly closed at address. This will allow the shoulders to turn further on the back swing, relative to the target line, thus producing more power, because, with the swing arc being greater, the club head is travelling faster at impact.

Never forget to align the club first, then your feet and body, and to check your grip. If you make a habit of setting up properly you will find you will play much better. Never rush a shot, never try to swing faster than normal.

You do, however, pull down hard with the hands on the down swing, rotating your hips and moving them laterally through the ball, your body turning to face the target as you finish.

Now to power driving.

Choosing the right driver for your swing is important, even if obvious. Metal heads are now very popular as they have a better weight distribution which creates a larger sweet spot; that leads to a better directed shot. Metal woods also have a lower centre of gravity, helping to hit the ball up into the air better than the traditional persimmon head. The metal headed driver I have used in the photographs is a MacGregor Jumbo with a larger head than usual. The loft is 9°.

Be careful in choosing the loft of your driver. They vary from about

The club only needs to pick up speed from the top of the back swing

You need to have the feeling that you are going through to hit a second ball

Metal woods, having a lower centre of gravity, do hit the ball higher

105

8.5° to 12°. It is probably better to use one around the top end of that scale. Even top tournament players use drivers with sufficient loft for their swing; José-Maria Olazábal uses a driver with a 10° face.

You must also buy a driver with the right flex shaft and the right size grip for your hands. Not everyone uses the same size golf gloves; not everyone should use the same size golf grip.

The ball position varies slightly with every player as some players reach the nadir of their swing earlier than others. Find your ideal ball position by trial and error.

On the Tee
The first thing to do on reaching the tee is to check the stroke index of the hole and the yardage. Then choose your target, but choose it carefully, not being too optimistic about carrying a bunker or other hazard at 240 yards if you normally only hit 250. Give yourself a 10% margin of error, more if there is a wind blowing. You may be better taking a 3-wood to lay up short of the hazard.

For now I am assuming we have a good, straight shot to a wide fairway, with no hazards or trees to worry about — bliss! Where is this golf club and can I join?

Tee the ball so that the top of the club is about level with the equator of the ball. If you tee it too low you may fade the ball, though more golfers tee too high than too low. Try teeing it slightly lower and see what happens,

More experienced golfers can add a few extra yards by standing very slightly closed at address with the driver. This has the effect of lengthening the back swing slightly.

particularly if you are using a metal headed driver.

Aim the club face exactly square to the chosen target and stand square to begin with. I have mentioned that, to get extra distance, you need to slightly draw the ball, moving it right to left in the air. It will help, in this, if you adjust your stance so that you are standing very slightly closed to the target. This has the effect of increasing the length of the back swing, relative to the ball-to-target line. This means that the club head is, in effect, beginning further back so has more time to pick up speed as it approaches the ball. Simple logic yet so often forgotten.

Your weight needs to be about 55-60% on your right side, so that your shoulders are tilting slightly, your right shoulder lower than your left by a couple of inches. Do make sure though, that they do not slide into an open position. Keep them a little closed to the target.

Don't tee too high, particularly with a metal headed driver. The top of the club should be no higher than the equator of the ball. You can also see from this photograph that the ball is just inside the left heel.

On the tee the first thing you should check is the stroke index of the hole, not the yardage

Tee the ball so that the top of the driver is about level with the equator of the ball

More experienced golfers can add a few yards to their drives by standing very slightly closed at address

There should be virtually a straight line from your left shoulder to the club head, though avoid being too stiff and rigid

Just as the outside of a wheel turns faster than the inside, so the club head moves faster than the hands

The late hit is a myth that traps many golfers; try to hit early, not late

There should be a virtually straight line from your left shoulder to the club head, your hands just behind the ball, though only just. Make sure that they are not in front of the ball on this shot. Now for a quick physics lesson.

I want you to think of a wheel turning. Although it is a single item, not hinged in any way but fixed in one piece, the outside is going faster than the inside. At a constant speed of, say, 60 rpm, the bigger the wheel the faster the outside edge is travelling.

The same applies to golf clubs. Swing a wedge and the club head will be travelling at a certain speed. Swing a driver at the same speed and the club head will be travelling faster, simply because the shaft is longer.

You do not, therefore, have to swing a driver any faster with your hands than you do a wedge. In fact, if you swing slightly slower you will still be bringing the club head into the ball much faster than with the wedge.

Forget about trying to swing faster with the driver.

On the take-away keep your left arm fairly straight though do not try to push the club back in a straight line. If you do that you are just pushing it outside the ball-to-target line and will have to swing back on the same plane, coming across the ball and slicing it.

I prefer, from a slightly closed stance, to allow the club to swing inside quite naturally. Check your grip, your right arm being a little relaxed and held in closer to your side than the left. The inside of your right elbow should be pointing away from your body and forwards, not into your body. Tuck that right elbow in slightly as

that will promote a more in-to-out swing, helping you to draw the ball, though be careful not to overdo it, particularly as we are standing slightly closed anyway.

The shoulders really must turn as much as possible on the back swing — failing to turn fully is one of the worst crimes a golfer can commit.

The downswing begins with the hips rotating to the left to make room for the arms to swing down and through. At the same time there is a transfer of weight towards the left side of the body that is as natural as water in a glass slopping from side to side as you move it.

Too many golfers try to throw their weight onto the left side, thus moving the body's pivot out of position too soon. The transfer of weight needs to be smooth and unhurried. Much is also made of kicking the right knee round toward the left, but if you do this too early you risk leaving the club head behind and pushing the ball straight right.

There is a myth about the late hit which can cause many of us problems. When you look at the swing sequence of Stephen Field, a European Tour player, you will see how far the club head is behind his hands on the way down into impact. His enormous hand power will bring the club head back square at impact.

He does not, however, deliberately hold back the uncocking of the wrists — it happens because of the way his weight is pulling the club head through impact.

Don't try to hold the club head back in this position. You will find that, on the contrary, if you try to

As the club is swung back
the right arm is nicely
tucked into the side of
the body. The eyes are
focused on the ball as
you can see even from
this angle.

At the top of the back
swing the shoulders must
really turn through 90° if
you want to produce
sufficient power.

Although the weight transfers left as the downswing begins you must not rush this, but let it happen as you pull down hard with your hands.

Just before impact the hands are still working hard to get the club head back square. Note how the weight has transferred to the left side.

After impact keep driving
the club head through,
trying to hit a second,
imaginary ball a couple of
feet further on.

The same moment from
a different angle.

You must never try to hit the ball up from the tee; it is sitting up and the driver has enough loft on it to do the job; just concentrate on hitting through the ball

Never quit on the shot, easing up before you actually hit the ball

pull your left arm straight from the elbow as you come down into the impact zone you will get the club head back square on time.

I would summarise this by telling you to forget the "late hit"; go for an "early hit" instead by ensuring you get your left arm straight at impact, as at address.

One very important aspect of power in driving, or any full shot for that matter, is the role of the hands. As the club head strikes the ball the right hand begins to roll across the left, known as the release. This is vital in producing power in the shot but avoid the feeling that you are somehow flicking at the ball, as you might if you were playing squash.

As you continue after impact there is a point, when the club and arms have reached about waist height on the follow-through, when the back of the right hand is vertical to the ground and parallel

Go for a complete follow-through, the body turning to face the target, the right knee kicking round. Although the ball has gone you must not stop.

to the target line. If you achieve this position — and check it in slow motion — it should prove that you have released the hands correctly.

At impact there are two main faults of less experienced golfers. The first is to think that the ball is all that matters; the second is that the ball has to be hit upwards with the driver. Both are wrong.

I have stated earlier that you should always feel that you have another ball to hit a foot or so in front of the real ball. In the first part of this course I used a club set into the ground, trying to hit the shaft on the follow-through. Having in mind that the ball is your target is rather like a runner just easing up a yard before the tape when he

112

is well in front of the field. He is "quitting" before crossing the finishing line.

A lot of golfers do the same. As you hit the ball you should still be accelerating the club. A very good practice tip to help you achieve the right feeling is to place two tees in the ground, one where the ball should be and a second one a foot in front of it, closer to the target. As you swing you must not only hit the "ball" on your first tee-peg, but also the second tee-peg as well. That will help you to sweep through the impact zone better. You can refine this even further by adding a third tee a foot or so behind the "ball", which you should knock out of the ground as you begin the back swing. That will tell you that you are taking the club away correctly rather than picking it up too steeply.

The second common error with the driver is that many golfers feel they have to hit the ball on the upswing.

The driver face is lofted — not much, but it is lofted. The loft on the driver face is what gets the ball airborne, not the way you hit it. You should feel that you are hitting straight along the ground as you hit the ball from the tee-peg. Never try to hit it upwards. Hit it straight and hit through as if you still had a second tee-peg in the ground a couple of inches beyond the ball.

You will find it useful, too, to attack the ball from very slightly inside the line, so that the club is actually travelling very slightly in-to-out across the ball at impact, which will promote a draw, thus adding extra distance to the shot. It is vital, though, that you do not overdo this, and that you continue driving the club head through impact rather than trying to pull it inside the line too quickly on the follow through.

The hands and wrists must flow through this shot so that you really feel "loose" and relaxed, not tight and wooden, which would just stifle the shot.

Played properly, the drive can be the most exciting shot in golf and it is one you can achieve quite easily, rather than getting frightened and tense every time you pull the driver out of the bag.

Use this club often, practising with it once you have warmed up with your other clubs, but always feel a genuine flowing movement through the ball, your arms pulling the club head through the impact position and the club pulling the body through with it.

If you tee the ball lower you will automatically sweep through the ball better than if you have it teed high, when you might be thinking of hitting it on the way up. Particularly with metal woods the ball will still be driven forwards, and in a better trajectory than if you try to hit it upwards.

Think for a moment of hitting a very short iron. The ball flies high but not far. The higher it goes, the shorter the shot. You want the drive to be long, so don't dissipate the energy of the ball by hitting it too high. Make sure that, as you hit the ball, the right shoulder is underneath the left, proof again that you are driving the club head through impact rather than merely pushing at it.

Two good practice routines will help you to swing the driver better and with more power in the shot rather than in the swing.

First, tape a 2-iron to your driver with strong tape — do make sure it

If you attack the ball from slightly inside you will find that you hit it further and with a little draw, which is the ideal shape of shot

If you tee the ball a little lower it may help you to sweep through it better as you will concentrate on keeping the club head low to the ground rather than trying to swing it upwards

By swinging two clubs together you will build up your golf muscles but more importantly will enhance your rhythm

Keep your left heel on the ground during the back swing

is strong or it might fly away as you swing. Grip both clubs together but don't worry too much about the correct grip as an overlapping grip here is very difficult to hold. Practice swinging and hitting a ball from the tee like this.

It slows your swing down and makes you transfer your weight more correctly. Do make sure that you come into the ball from very slightly inside the line. This is a wonderful exercise.

The second exercise is to hold, with both hands, a bag of practice balls — not too heavy, just about 30 balls in the bag. Stand as you would to hit a shot and have a target in mind about 20 feet away. Swing back and then through, throwing the bag to your target. Your body will turn as you throw the bag, to face the target just as you should with a golf shot. This will help you to realise that golf is really just a set of very natural movements, not a game for contortionists as some people try to make out.

I have not yet mentioned the

role of the legs and feet in the swing because they play no independent part, yet as they support the body they are an integral part of the entire swing.

My personal feeling is that, if you want power in your shots, your left heel should stay on the ground throughout the swing. Many higher handicap golfers lift their left heel off the ground in the back swing. Don't.

There is also a tendency among many golfers to kick the right knee out on the downswing, away from the body. It must kick left, the right foot moving to a tip-toe position at the finish. The left leg should also finish almost straight rather than bent at the knee.

A great exercise to help you turn, transfer your weight and release your hands correctly. Hold a bag of practice balls, swing it back as you would a club, then throw it to a target about 20 feet away. To get it straight you have to turn fully and release it from your hands at the correct moment, setting it off at the right angle.

Don't let your right knee collapse forwards during the swing. It needs to kick round to the left, though if you do it too early you will block the shot.

Now for the other long shots you will need and I must begin by suggesting that you learn how to use a set of golf clubs properly. Please don't think I am being facetious but you will find that many golfers, although they carry fourteen clubs, don't get the full value out of each one. Ignoring the putter, do you hit thirteen different distances with your other clubs? With the irons the general rule is that each one should give you an extra ten yards or so in distance and whilst this may be true with your shorter irons, the average golfer does not get an extra ten yards with the longer irons. Indeed, many golfers can hit a 5-iron the same distance they do a 3-iron.

The main problem is that they tend to hit at the ball rather than through it; it really is that simple.

I have mentioned earlier that you must have the feeling that there is a second ball to hit a couple of feet in front of you. Sweep the club through to that imaginary target and you are on the way to becoming a better golfer.

There is also a mental problem with the longer irons. From the 5-iron to the wedge the aim is accuracy. From the 4-iron to the driver you are looking for distance and as much accuracy as possible, though you should be content to get the ball a decent distance and not too far off track.

You need to practise with the long irons on a regular basis, though don't use them from a poor lie.

Fairway woods, the 5 and 3, are easy to use provided you set up correctly and, once again, sweep the ball away rather than hitting at it. Have the ball more towards the front of your stance but not too far forward. Experiment with the ball position to find the one that suits your swing best. Always turn your shoulders fully and keep your head behind the ball all the time, getting the arms straight at impact. Attack the ball from very slightly inside the line but have this feeling that you have a second target — like a tee-peg — a couple of inches ahead of the ball and you must hit that with your maximum power.

Once again your right shoulder will be under the left at impact as the body weight is transferring to the left side. Your head should stay over the back of the ball until after impact.

Release your hands going through so that your right hand is vertical halfway up in the follow-through and parallel to the target line.

Although you have fourteen clubs you may not be getting the best value from them; try to get the best out of each club but understand what their uses are

Fairway woods need to be swept through the ball and this is good practice for the long irons too, which need to be swept smoothly

Always attack the ball from slightly inside

The drive, in sequence.

Top: From a balanced address position the club is taken away low, with the left arm fairly straight. At the top of the back swing the shoulders have fully turned, the back pointing at the target. The downswing begins with the weight transferring left and the hands pulling down hard on the club.

Below: At impact the hands have returned the club to its square position and the right knee is kicking left as the right shoulder comes under and through impact, continuing to turn as the weight sweeps the club through to a balanced finish, the body turning to face the target.

Stephen Field of the European PGA Tour demonstrates his power in this driving sequence.

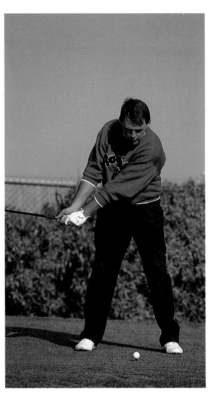

Stephen Field again, from the other angle. Follow this and you won't go far wrong.

The Scoring Zone

Hitting the ball long distances is very rewarding but you need to remember that over 60% of the shots in an average round of golf are played from within 100 yards of the pin.

Ignoring those that are played on the green itself you can still see that the short game is vital if you are to score well.

There will inevitably be some par-4 holes where only the very longest hitters can reach the green in two shots, particularly if into a wind or on fairways that are uphill. You may even hit a slightly wayward second shot, missing the green by a few yards and landing in an area of semi-rough to one side.

It is then vital to hit your short approach to within a single putt distance of the pin if you are to save par.

There will also be many par-5s where you can almost reach the green with your second shot as you become more experienced, yet you are still left with a delicate little shot of, maybe, 60 yards or so to the green.

Getting that approach shot very close to the pin can set up a birdie.

If you can get the ball stone dead in these situations you will lower your scores dramatically. What I want to do now is to take you through some of the situations you may encounter and show you how to play them.

I will start by just suggesting that you fully understand that the short clubs are for accuracy rather than length. I normally hit a 7-iron about 135 yards but if I have an approach to the green of 137 yards I would never think of trying to hit

the 7-iron an extra two yards. It's easier to take the 6-iron, grip down the club very slightly and hit it at 90%. That has to be easier than trying to hit the 7-iron 105% ! So many times I see golfers trying to do things they really should not attempt and I cannot stress strongly enough that you should play the shots you can hit nine times out of ten, not those you can only play one-in-ten.

Learn how far you hit each club; actually make a note of it in a little book and recheck it every couple of months as the seasons change. In the winter a golf ball flies less distance, just as it does when it's wet or humid.

I have, in this course of lessons, often mentioned yards. Many countries use metres and as a rough guide deduct 10% from yards to get metres. A shot of 100 yards roughly equates to 90 metres.

If you are working in metres, or see a scorecard with metres, add 10% to get yards. A shot of 150 metres is about 165 yards.

I shall deal first with shots to greens at a different level, either elevated, from where you are, or down in a dip. The illustration over the page clearly shows the trajectory of a ball to a green on the same level, one on a higher level and one on a lower level.

Greg Norman floats another short approach shot to a couple of feet from the pin, setting up another birdie opportunity. The ability of professionals to play these shots with such accuracy is merely a reflection on the amount of care they take — and the amount of practice they put in!

Even if you are not accurate with your long shots, skill in the short game will save par on a regular basis

---

Understand how far you hit each club, with both a draw and a fade

---

Although, when you look at this it is fairly obvious that you need more club to hit to the higher green than the lower, so many golfers fail to take this simple fact into a account, merely looking at the distance and hitting the appropriate club.

In the example I have shown I am assuming that you would need a 7-iron for the shot to the level green. That would make the shot to the elevated green a 6-iron; that to the lower green maybe an 8-iron.

At La Manga the shot from the tee of a downhill par-3 needed a 9-iron for a distance of 134 yards. On level ground that is about a 7-iron for me.

Whilst on the subject of shots to a different level green let me deal with those delicate little shots around the green where you either have to hit the ball up to a green from a position below it, or to hit the ball down to a green from off a bank.

First, the shot from below the level of the green. In this instance the ball had to be hit up over a bunker to the green and one of the biggest problems is that you cannot see the base of the flag.

The first thing to do is to walk

Club	From	To
Wedge	60	110
9	110	120
8	120	135
7	135	145
6	145	155
5	155	165
4	165	175
3	175	185
2	185	190

Make a note of how far you hit each club. Warm up first, then hit about six to ten balls with each club, taking the average distance — never the best, never the worst. Always aim at a specific target, like an umbrella stuck in the ground or something you can see clearly. The distances will vary quite a lot from season to season, so re-measure them every couple of months.

If you are hitting to an elevated green the ball reaches the green earlier in its flight, so it has not travelled so far. To reach the pin you need to take more club. Hitting to a green below you the ball will travel further before it reaches the surface, so you need less club.

It should be obvious but if you hit a ball downhill it goes further; if you hit uphill it goes less distance

Always look carefully at the slopes around the green as you want to put the ball in the best possible position for your next shot

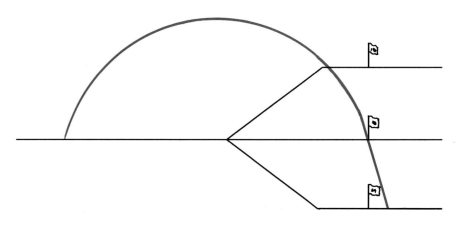

The first thing to do is to look at the green to see if you need to land the ball above the pin to take advantage of any slope — the ball always rolls downhill.

Next, set up fairly open, take a half back swing — just enough to generate the correct power — and then hit hard — but slowly — under the ball, lifting it well. If it has height it will stop on landing, more so with a balata ball. You should follow through a greater distance than the back swing — remember 45% back; 55% through.

up to the green and take a careful look around. If you were putting on the green you would want to know where the slopes were, if any, and how far on the green the hole was cut. You need the same information now.

Look around and check carefully before deciding where the ball should land to allow it to roll gently towards the hole. It will always roll downhill on a sloping green so allow for that. It's obvious I know, yet many people forget it, or perhaps ignore it.

Because the ball was sitting up fairly well in fluffy grass I could hit a sand wedge quite easily on this occasion. Set up fairly open with the ball central in your stance, take a three-quarter swing — but slow — and swing through the ball, lifting it with a fairly wristy swing but a good follow-through, though never trying to scoop it. If you want the ball to rise you need to punch the club into the grass bank, the loft on the club face is what lifts the ball up. You do not need to cut off the follow-through as the ball is rising fairly steeply so will stop quickly once it lands.

Only if it will not rise too much should you think of cutting off the follow-through.

With this delicate downhill pitch it would be impossible to carry the bunker and stop the ball on the green; I know, I tried it! The sensible option is to play to the fat part of the green using a sand wedge and a very open stance. Cut off the follow-through by keeping the club face pointing skywards at the end of the shot. I also pull the hands further round the body to the left. The ball must land on the edge of the green — don't leave it short.

Play to the fat of the green when going at the pin is likely to be dangerous; you get no prizes for attempting the impossible

Try to get the rhythm of your swing right on your short shots, but never quit on the shot, keeping your hands ahead of the club head at all times

Although there is a lot of pressure to speed up your golf I really think you should take more time on your shots. Hurry between shots by all means, but never be rushed into making a mistake; you only get one chance

You can be calmly aggressive if you have a lot of green to work with

Do, however, take the time to walk up to the green to check carefully where you want the ball to land — this again is one of those instances where I must urge you not to hurry. If you do that you may waste a shot.

Nothing is worse in golf than being hurried into making the wrong shot. By all means rush between shots and get yourself ready to play whilst your partners are taking their shots (without distracting them of course), but never rush your own shots.

Shots from off a bank to a lower level green are far more delicate.

Again I would favour the sand wedge as it can put more backspin on the ball than any other club. The situation on this shot was that to reach the pin the ball had to fly across a bunker, and stop quickly.

From where I was that was clearly impossible so the sensible option was to play to the safe part of the green, leaving a long putt but the ball was on the putting surface.

The hands are set almost vertically above the ball — not in front and definitely not behind. The stance is very open but the club face is pointing at the target I have chosen — the fat of the green.

The back swing is virtually non-existent, just a very gentle take-away from the ball before sliding the blade under the ball as delicately as possible.

Here the follow-through is held, the club only going forward a very small distance. Again, to help cut it off and slice the ball even more, stopping it on landing as well as turning it towards the pin as it lands, I have pulled the club round to the left of the body.

One important point on this shot is to ensure that you land the

ball where you want it, in this case on the fringe. Don't land it in the grass further down the slope because that might stop the ball and you have wasted a shot. Be calmly aggressive and land the ball on the putting surface. Never under-hit this shot.

Another sloping lie is that where you are just off the green on a downslope of light semi-rough. Here the ball is played back in the stance, almost off the right toe, the hands ahead of the ball. Note how close together the feet are, as you want virtually no lower body or leg movement on this delicate shot.

Again I favour the sand wedge, though if there is a lot of green to work with the wedge is possibly better. If the green is wet I might even use a 9-iron to get extra roll. At La Manga the greens were fairly fast and exceptionally true.

Although the hands are ahead of the ball note carefully how the head is behind it. This really is one of golf's golden rules — always keep the head behind the ball.

The back swing is very short and less wristy than normal as I am just trying to slide the club face under the ball and get it airborne. That will allow it to jump onto the green about midway between me and the flag and roll the rest of the way. There is no wrist-cock on the back swing as the arms and hands take the club away in one movement, as on a putt.

The photograph just after impact shows how quickly the ball is rising off the club face, so that when it lands it will not run too far. The follow-through is severely

This is a shot many players leave short, down a slope and across a reasonable amount of green.

The stance is very open and the hands are well ahead of the ball at address. Because you are on a slope don't forget to adjust your weight slightly, though it does not show so much as on a fuller swing. The back swing is very short, again just sufficient to allow you to accelerate the club through the impact zone. It tends to be a little more wristy because you want extra "feel" in the shot. The club face gets right under the ball lifting it quickly — again it is so important to get the ball in the air rather than just rolling it down the slope, a mistake too many golfers make. You can see that there is little follow-through, the club face finishing pointing to the sky.

On short shots in particular you must keep your hands ahead of the club head and the ball at impact, but your head behind it

Although there is not so much body movement in the short game you must not stand stiff and wooden

cut off to restrict its distance. Even at impact the hands are still ahead of the ball, but the head is not.

The sand wedge is the ideal club for these shots but I must warn you against using it off a hard fairway or area of ground with little grass as its heavy flange will just bounce off the hard surface and you will thin the shot you are attempting. If you need height on the ball use a wedge; if you just need to knock the ball forward, take something like an 8-iron.

In the earlier part of this course we did look at chipping the ball onto the green. I now want to take you through the perfect way to do this with Stephen Field, a European Tour player.

The situation here is a shot from just off the green, slightly uphill and with no more than 15 yards to the pin. From the ball to the edge of the green is about five yards. The ball is sitting up fairly well and Stephen is using a sand wedge.

The address position has the ball about central in a slightly open stance but note how the hands are well forward of the ball, the head held perfectly above the back of the ball. As I have mentioned before the head should always stay behind the ball.

The feet are fairly close together as there is little body movement on this shot, though you never stand like a statue — golf is an athletic game requiring movement, but you don't need to be an Olympic sprinter to play well.

The back swing is fairly short, the hands only just reaching waist high but Stephen uses his hands to good effect, getting the club back a little further. That allows him to bring the hands through well ahead of the ball — look at the difference between this picture and the address — and, with a wristy shot, lift the ball fairly steeply away from the ground. That will get it floating onto the green where it

will roll nicely to the pin, setting up a single putt.

Far too many golfers are afraid of this delicate little shot and I have seen hundreds of golfers in this position just tap the ball forward with a wedge, then wonder why it has stopped short of the pin or run on past.

The professionals are so good at the short game and this really does make a vast difference to your scoring capabilities. If you can practise shots like this, trying things you have never done before, you will improve your golf. You can control the ball if you understand how it reacts to being hit, and how it rolls.

The place to perfect these shots is, though, on the practice ground, not out on the course.

Before we leave the short game, which is arguably the most important aspect of golf I would just like to take you through the various circumstances under which

you play a particular shot, and briefly how to play them. Use this as a reference.

For shots from just off the green where you have no problems in front of you, you have a choice of either a long putt or a delicate chip and run. If you are only just off the edge of the green a putt might be the best choice, but I would hesitate about using the putter from anything more than about four yards from the edge of the green unless the grass was bone dry and very, very short.

To putt a long way take the putter head back inside the line, as you would for a normal shot. In this instance forget about trying to keep the putter straight as you go back. Set up square to the target with the ball slightly forward of centre in your stance, take the putter back gently but just inside the line and try to hit the ball on its equator, following through completely with the back of your

If you want the ball to shop quickly, keep your hands and wrists firm throughout the shot, so that you finish with the back of your left hand facing the target; if you want the ball to run just gently release your hands as you come through impact

left hand and the putter face finishing pointing straight at the target, taking any borrow into account, naturally.

From a little further back, but again with a straight approach with no hazards in the way, something like a 7-iron could be your best bet, playing it very much like a long putt, exactly as with the putter just a moment ago. The loft on the club face will get the ball airborne enough to fly over the intervening grass between you and the green and land the ball safely on the putting surface. To ensure the ball continues rolling once it lands, for a pin cut on the far side of the green, for example, release your hands after impact so that the back of the right hand finishes vertical to the ground and pointing directly at the target.

If you want the ball to stop fairly short from this position consider using a more lofted iron such as a 9-iron or wedge. The shorter the

shot the more lofted the iron, obvious once again but you see so many golfers trying to play short shots with just one club rather than using a different one for each situation. If you are to get full value from your set of clubs — which are not cheap — you should learn to play every type of shot with each club. That will make you a real shot-maker.

As you move further back you need to get the ball in the air more to safely fly to the green and here the more lofted clubs such as the wedge and sand wedge come into their own.

Remember that, if you want the ball to stop quickly on landing you must cut off the follow-through, holding the back of the left hand pointing at the target at the finish; if you want the ball to run release your hands through impact.

To fly the ball over a bunker you do not always have to use a wedge, though that is what most golfers

From a narrow stance . . .

the club is taken back halfway.

favour. Be more adventurous and try the 7-iron, particularly if the pin is on the far side of the green. Too often I see players hitting the ball nicely over the bunker on to the green but then, because they have used the sand wedge for maximum height, to avoid dropping into the bunker, landing the ball well short of the flag and needing two putts to get down.

The 7-iron will, if you hit it just as on that earlier approach from a few yards off the green, get the ball airborne to fly the bunker and land on the green. Unlike the wedge, the shot from the 7-iron will then run, getting much closer to the hole and setting up a single putt. After all it doesn't matter whether the ball clears the bunker by two feet or ten feet — it only has to clear it by a safe margin.

Many players fear hitting a 7-iron from this distance, but if you strike the ball correctly, using a narrow, open stance and swinging slowly through the ball, remembering always to keep accelerating through impact, you will get the ball safely on the green, and near the hole, every time.

Earlier in this course of lessons I covered hitting the ball over a lake and I would just like to mention that again here, for it applies also to an approach shot of, say, 100 yards or so when you know you need to get the ball safely on the green. If the pin is cut close to the front edge of the green it would be futile attempting to land the ball very close to the hole. A better idea is to look at the back of the green, or the fat of the green, and aim for that. Play safe, unless you are in a do-or-die situation in matchplay with your opponent on the green.

Short shots are the ones which score and I must confess that this is the area of your game you should practise more often if you are to improve your scores in the shortest possible time.

Going over a bunker just in front of the green is fairly easy though many players hit it too high and leave it short. Hit it just high enough to safely clear the hazard, then let it roll to the pin; that way you will end up with fewer putts and a lower score

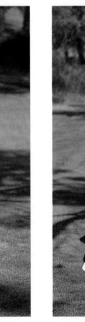 

The head stays behind the ball . . .   as the club is swung through.

Get Out of Trouble Fast

Not every shot you play will be from the middle of a perfectly flat fairway. There are times when even the best players land slightly off the fairway itself, leaving awkward shots which might need to be shaped or perhaps hit high over, or low under, some trees between you and the green. Even if you are on the fairway it may not be flat and you may have to play either uphill or down, or from the awkward lies with the ball above or below your feet.

Then there are shots from rough just around the green, where you need to get the ball safely out, but then control it rather than have it run through the green into perhaps more trouble.

In the first part of this course I dealt with playing from rough and semi-rough when you have sufficient room to hit a full shot.

I would just reiterate that your main aim is to get out of the rough first time and a lofted club may well be the most sensible choice, placing the shot to where you can hit a good next shot rather than just going for distance.

Address the ball in about the centre of your stance with your hands pressed slightly ahead of the ball and your weight favouring your left side, enabling you to take the club away fairly steeply and then hitting down hard and through the ball, moving your weight firmly onto your left side.

Seve Ballesteros has always had a marvellous capacity to manufacture shots in the most difficult conditions. Knowing your capabilities helps as you must never attempt the impossible.

Sloping Lies

As you know not all fairways are flat so you need to understand how to adjust your position to compensate for any slopes you may be standing on. I will deal first with uphill lies, where you are hitting the ball up a slope.

Uphill Lies

Nature dictates your stance, for if you just stand on a slope you will see that your weight is more supported on your lower side, your higher side flexing more to get your body back to level with gravity, rather like a spirit level.

To play a golf shot from an upslope, you are standing with your right leg further down the slope. This does, therefore, take more of the weight of your body. There is nothing you can do to change this, it just happens.

When you are in deep rough you really must hit through the ball hard, with your weight moving well to the left side.

You should practise playing from rough and other awkward situations fairly regularly; then, if you do stray off the fairway you will know what you need to do to get the ball back in play

On a sloping lie never try to be too clever — just play sensibly

What you want to do is to set your shoulders parallel to the slope so that you are, in effect, standing flat.

Because you are standing on a slope the natural reaction of the body is to level itself against gravity, in effect fighting the slope, particularly as you swing down into the ball. You will, whether you like it or not, thus be hitting the ground relatively earlier in your swing, with a relatively steeper downswing. That has the effect of punching the ball away more, rather than sweeping through it. It is easier to play a punch shot with a shorter iron. Try to keep the feeling that you are hitting uphill rather than coming down into the back of the ball, so that, as you swing back you take a wider arc and keep the ball swinging along the contours of the slope as long as possible.

Because you are hitting the ball earlier it needs to be slightly further back in your stance than normal, probably about the centre of your stance for this shot — I am using a 6-iron here, with 130 yards to the green.

Just as nature has given you your stance, nature, with the aid of gravity, will try to pull you out of position on the back swing because, as you swing back your weight transfers to the right side. In this case the right side is further down the slope, so your weight will try to topple you over. This you must resist so never swing more than three-quarters at most. You also don't want to transfer any more weight than you have to, so keep your left foot firmly planted on the ground as you swing back. Do avoid a reverse pivot though — turn your shoulders.

As you swing through impact

When hitting uphill try to really push your right leg into the shot, so that you are driving your body up the slope as well as the ball. You should always stand a little closed for this shot and aim more right as the ball will always draw

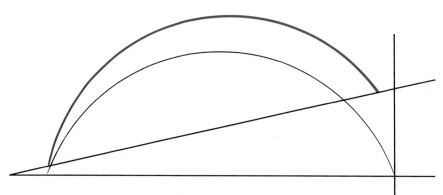

When you hit from an uphill lie the ball will follow the same trajectory as it would for that club, but you need to take into account the slope. The black line shows the ball trajectory for a 6-iron from a flat lie. The red line above it shows how the ball will travel if hit from an upslope. The trajectories are the same (allowing a slight variation for the effects of gravity on the shot hit from the upslope), though the ball from the upslope will appear to fly lower. They also appear to travel the same distance, though in truth the ball from the upslope will travel slightly less, due to the slightly greater effects of gravity. However, don't let all this technical language worry you as the important things to realise is that, when hitting uphill, you need more club and when hitting downhill, less club. What could be easier to remember?

Your shoulder line must be parallel to the slope, always putting extra weight on the leg lower down the slope.

You must be very careful not to let your weight topple back as you swing, which is why I suggest a three-quarter swing with nothing more than a mid-iron. Never use a wood on this shot, however far you are from the green.

keep moving through the ball, turning your hips out of the way and finish your follow-through. To get extra power and direction into this shot drive your body up the slope more, using your right leg to push you uphill.

Because the ball is back in your stance and you are hitting relatively earlier, you will need to stand slightly closed on this shot, aiming slightly right of your target. The ball will be drawn round to the left in mid-air.

Another consequence of hitting uphill is that the loft of the club is increased relative to gravity. A 6-iron thus takes on the characteristics of a 7-iron or maybe even an 8, depending on the severity of the slope. As I said I have here a shot of 130 yards which would normally need an easy 7-iron,

but the stance and effective loft dictate that a 6-iron should be used.

Downhill Lies

What goes up must come down so if you have an uphill lie you are more than likely to, at some time, have a downhill lie.

Nature again gives you the setup, your weight automatically being supported on the side lower down the slope, this time your left. Once again, set your shoulders parallel to the slope, play the ball in the centre of your stance and avoid anything longer than a 5-iron. On not too severe a downslope I would consider playing a wood if there was a bunker or other hazard in front of the green which I need to carry, as an iron hit off a downslope,

Going downhill you may well lose your balance as you hit the ball but guard against trying to hit too hard. Stand slightly open as you will always fade the ball going downhill. It is always difficult to fly it over a bunker or other hazard close to the green so avoid the temptation of going straight at the pin unless it is safe to do

Once again your shoulder line is parallel to the slope.

Set up with your hands fairly well ahead of the ball which is further back in your stance than on a level fairway.

140

particularly one longer than about an 7-iron, will stay fairly low, taking on the loft characteristics of one or two clubs stronger, so a 7-iron takes on the loft of a 5-iron, for example. It will, however, hit it further so if you normally hit a 7-iron 130 yards, take an 8-iron downhill for the same distance.

With a reasonable distance and a bunker or other hazard to carry in front of the green the 5-wood, which can even be used out of the semi-rough, will get the ball high and give it sufficient distance. You can also work a 5-wood, shaping the shot better than you can a 5-iron, for example.

Hitting downhill you need to stand slightly open to the target and aim slightly left, as the ball will tend to fade into the green from a down slope. Again keep the ball in the centre of your stance but remember to follow your weight through the impact zone rather than holding back. If you hold your weight back your head and arms will come up too quickly on the follow-through and you may top the ball, merely sending it scuttling downhill. Although it may still reach its target it is not the shot you want to play.

Side Lies
These often cause problems to less experienced golfers but are really quite simple. You will either have the ball above your feet or below your feet. I shall deal with the ball above your feet first.

If you walk up a hill you will notice that you lean your body into the slope, balancing more on your toes, once again setting yourself

Side lies can be difficult but if you adjust your stance and only hit with a three-quarter swing you won't go far wrong

Don't overswing although because you are not standing level your swing might seem longer than normal.

You are quite likely to lose your balance as you swing through on this shot. Try to hold it on the back swing but just follow nature on the follow-through.

With the ball above your feet, you are closer to the ball so you need to stand slightly taller and grip down the club for more control. Always aim up the slope as the ball will follow gravity

With the ball below your feet you may need to bend over slightly, but do this by flexing your knees more rather than stooping over the ball; aim up the slope again as the ball will always follow gravity

level so that your centre of gravity is vertical in relation to flat ground, not to the slope. If you stood at 90° to the slope, as you do to flat ground, you would fall over backwards. Nature will not allow you to do it.

Your stance on a slope, with the ball above your feet, means, then, that you are leaning forwards into the slope. We have seen earlier that your spine should be fairly straight, your body bending at the hips and knees. Because of the situation you are now in you will have your knees and hips more upright, so that you are almost standing up straight.

This brings the ball nearer to your body so you need to grip well down the club. The ball, like everything else, will follow gravity so if you just knocked it forward ten yards it would roll down the hill, moving right to left on your target line. It will do the same if you hit it 110 yards.

For these two reasons you should aim the club face, and your feet, to the right of the target. The ball will come round in the air and, if you have your calculations right, will reach the target. Don't forget that a ball moving right to left in mid air will travel further than one travelling straight, so allow for that, taking less club if necessary though as you are gripping down the club you are reducing the length of the swing and thus the distance.

Swing more with your shoulders and arms, with less lower body movement.

With the ball below your feet nature again dictates your stance, and here you would be balancing your weight more on your heels or you would fall forwards.

Hold the club as long as you

can, right to the end of the grip and have the ball in the centre of your stance. Try not to stoop too much, still keeping your spine as straight as you can.

The ball will follow gravity, rolling left to right, so set up aiming well left of your target. The ball will fade round into position. It will travel less distance than one hit from a flat lie, so take more club, though never much more than about a 5-iron.

To summarise then, on all sloping lies, let nature dictate your stance; keep in mind that the ball will follow gravity so aim to one side as necessary; never take more than a 5-iron; swing slowly, keeping your lower body still and swinging more with your arms and shoulders. Keep the swing slow and smooth.

Trees
Trees are a beautiful addition to golf courses — indeed most trees were there long before the golf course. For golfers unfortunate enough to have strayed off the straight and narrow they can, however, be a hazard.

Although trees are something like 80% air, it is rather difficult, particularly in summer when they are in full bloom, to drive the ball through the branches and leaves without hitting something. The only real options, then, are to go round, under or over the tree, missing all the potential trouble.

Going over is quite simple, providing you are far enough back from the tree and have enough club to hit the ball over the top safely. To get the ball airborne quickly play it slightly more forward in your stance than normal, between the middle of the

Because the ball will follow gravity you must aim it higher up the slope, but don't close the club face.

The ball will follow gravity so aim it up the slope, but don't stand open — stand square to your first target.

stance and the left instep. Stand with a more open stance than normal, so that the club face appears more open (i.e. it is laid more horizontal than normal, though the bottom groove is still pointing directly at your target). This, and the ball position, will help you to get more loft on the ball, hitting it higher, though you must guard against falling back on the shot in an attempt to hit it higher. The loft on the club face and the ball position will do that as they do on every other shot. Never try to scoop the ball.

You do, however, lose distance so if you still want to get the ball a specific distance, take more club, a 5- rather than a 7-iron, for example. I wouldn't use a longer iron than this, though again the little 5-wood could be the ideal club, providing you are far enough back from the tree as you cannot increase the loft on the 5-wood

You can check whether you have enough loft to get over a tree by laying a club with the blade flat on the ground. If the shaft points above the tree you have.

To hit the ball high set up a little open, the ball further forward in your stance

except by deliberately slicing the ball.

To do this with the 5-wood, aim the club face at the target but stand well open. Have the ball in the middle of your stance and hit normally and smoothly. You might find it useful to grip down slightly on these shots, with both the irons and the 5-wood. That forces you into making a more wristy release through the ball and will help to get the ball airborne.

Going under the tree you need to keep the ball low. To do this play it further back in your stance

but with your hands held in their normal address position. This hoods the club face, turning it over and delofting it. Make sure you do not close the face by pointing the toe in too much.

Use one of the long irons if possible as they have less loft to begin with. The shot needs to be a straight punch, cutting of the follow through with the hands

Then stand slightly open, so that the club face is slightly more horizontal, though still pointing at the target, and swing as normal.

To hit the ball lower, stand slightly closed with the ball back in your stance; a longer iron, with less loft on it, is the ideal club to use, gripping on it for better control

To keep the ball low, cut off your follow-through so that your hands and wrists remain firm, the back of your left hand pointing at the target

To keep it low hood the face by having the ball well back in your stance . . .

If you have a difficult shot look for the easy option; at the end of your round you are not asked how you played the shots, but how many shots you took

. . . and cut off the follow-through, which will drive the ball forward a good distance and keep it under the branches.

coming through without releasing.

This means that as you finish the shot your arms are both straight and finish about waist high, the back of the left hand still pointing skywards. Make sure you hit fairly hard through the ball rather than just tapping at it. It must be a proper shot.

If you are ever unsure of what club to use you can easily check the angle of elevation the ball will take.

To do this place the club you intend using — I used a 4-iron for the photograph below — and stand (gently!) on the face, though to show it better in the photograph I have placed my hand on it. The shaft will show you at what angle of elevation the ball will leave the club face. You can then judge whether it will stay low enough to miss the branches or not.

You can keep it slightly lower by hooding the face, the ball well back in your stance, but keep in mind that in doing that you will hook the ball a little, so compensate by aiming more to the right if you can.

When playing Commonwealth Golf Club in Melbourne once I had this type of situation, having hit my approach under a tree just 20 yards

This was a really difficult situation, with the ball under a low branch of the tree, a steep bunker between the ball and green and out-of-bounds at the back of the green. It was not possible to get enough height on the ball to carry the bunker and stay on the green. One option was to hit the ball into the bunker, hoping to get up and down from there, but after careful reflection it was more sensible to play out sideways onto the approach to the green and chip the ball to the pin. This was what I did, dropping just one stroke instead of maybe more.

from the green. There was no room to get the ball airborne more than about three feet, but I couldn't run it straight at the green because of a huge, deep bunker between the ball and the green.

To make matters worse the green sloped away from me with out-of-bounds across the other side of the green. There were really two options. First, to hood a 6-iron, gripping right down and to knock the ball forward into the bunker (it was impossible to get over the lip of the bunker and stop the ball on the green), taking the chance of getting up and down from the sand; secondly to play out sideways to leave a straightforward chip and run to a position on the green close enough to single putt. Either way it was going to be three strokes from there. I played the second, safer option, dropping a stroke to par — but only one.

Going round the tree is, in many ways, easier because you have only to hook, or slice the ball. To hook the ball, play it back in your stance and aim the club face at your real target. Close your feet and body stance, aiming them well right of the target, at least far enough right to miss the tree.

Swing fully with a good shoulder turn and hit through the shot. That will start the ball right of the tree and bring it round left in the air. A hooked shot will normally travel further so take one club less than you would normally need for the distance you have left.

To hook the ball round the trees have it fairly well back in your stance, aim the club face at your real target (where you want it to finish) and then stand closed. The ball will start on your feet line but then hook to the club face line.

When you hook or draw a shot it will normally go further; when you fade or slice the ball it will travel less distance. Adjust the strength of your shots accordingly, using the clubs to suit the conditions and the situations you have

To slice a shot do the opposite. Stand well open to the target, but again with the club face aiming at the target. Have the ball slightly forward in your stance but not too much or you risk topping it. Swing fully and the ball will start left of the tree and turn right in mid air.

A sliced shot normally goes less distance than one hit straight so take more club than you need. If you have a long way to go this is the perfect situation in which to use a driver off the fairway. It sounds difficult but is not. Have the ball in the middle of your stance as you would for a 5-wood, stand open and swing normally.

You will keep the ball fairly low with this shot — ideal if you want to stay under branches as well as go slightly left of them — and will travel easily some 170 yards or so.

It's a very effective shot and I

To slice a ball stand more open with the ball forward in your stance

strongly suggest you practice using the driver off the fairway to see what distance and shape you will get from it. It will also help straighten up your drives as it forces you to hit through the ball rather than trying to scoop it. I have mentioned this again in the section on driving.

There is one further problem area you are likely to encounter with trees and that is when your

ball is in the trees — not literally, although it has happened that a ball has stuck in a tree and the only option is to climb the tree and try to hit it (which both Langer and Faldo have done in tournaments to

To slice the ball round the tree aim the club face at your real target, open your stance and the ball will start at your feet line target and then move round to the club face target.

To draw the ball stand slightly closed with the ball further back in your stance

my knowledge) or to declare it
unplayable and take a penalty
drop, which I have had to do once.
You would be very unfortunate to
land the ball in the tree itself. Far
more likely is that the ball will be
on the ground below the trees.

In this situation your sole aim is
to get the ball back out onto the
fairway from where you can have a
safe shot next time. Aiming the ball
through gaps in the trees is easy, so
long as you find a gap that is big
enough and then aim the club face
to get the ball through it.

In the situation in the photographs I had 190 yards to the green
but it was a slight dog-leg to the
left. There was, therefore, no
possibility of reaching the green;
the direct line forward out of the
trees involved getting through a
very narrow gap, so my only
sensible option was to hit the ball

To get the ball out further down the
fairway would have meant missing the
tree growing at an angle and the other
trees. Frankly, the gap was too small.
The sensible option was to hit the ball
to the other side of the fairway almost
opposite me, getting it well clear of the
tree line and leaving me a clear shot
into the green.

I used a 6-iron, the ball well back in
my stance. The club face must be
aligned perfectly to get through the
gap. A very short back swing is just
enough to accelerate the club head
through the ball, getting it off the
ground with enough power to get it
across the fairway and no more. The
cut off follow-through will stop it in the
correct place.

152

to the opposite side of the fairway, giving me a straight line into the green and the loss of only one shot — though if the approach was on target I might even make it with a single putt.

To keep it low I took a 6-iron, played the ball well back in my stance with the hands pressed well forward, hooding the club face and just punched it out low, with a minimum back swing and a cut-off follow through. Because there is little back swing the club face hardly gets off line and it is almost like a long putt. You do need to make sure the ball will rise sufficiently to clear any debris on the ground though, so do hit through it, albeit rather gently.

Wind and Rain
Finally, before we leave trouble shots, two situations which I regularly find myself trying to play golf in — wind and rain. Unless you are lucky enough to live in a land of perpetual sunshine you will be faced with battling against these elements as well as the golf course itself from time to time.

I must say that the most

A fairway wood is probably better from a wet fairway as it will sweep through the shot rather than digging in. After all, you never take a divot with a fairway wood.

When the greens are wet you can be more aggressive, flying the ball directly at the pin.

terrifying golf course I have played in strong wind — actually it was a howling gale! — was Royal Portrush in Ireland. If you have played it you'll know why. Tralee, Waterville and Ballybunion in strong wind are not far behind.

In a headwind you want, if possible, to keep the ball low, particularly for longer shots. To drive a good distance, tee the ball as normal but address the ball with the driver slightly higher than usual. You want to hit the ball halfway up rather than square on. This, in effect, tops it slightly but still hits it the correct distance, boring it low under the wind. You might want to have the ball slightly further forward in your stance but don't overdo it or you will thin it or slice it. You might find it better, also, to stand slightly closed for this shot which helps to keep it lower.

Into the wind you can keep the drive long and low by hitting the ball with the base of the club halfway up the ball. This slightly tops it and keeps it low but on line.

> On a long shot in a cross wind use the wind, aiming into it to begin with and letting the ball work back to the target; on short shots do the opposite, playing the ball against the wind so that you can control it as it hits the green

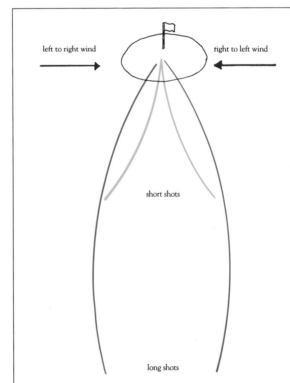

left to right wind   right to left wind

short shots

long shots

To understand how to work the ball in cross winds, use this illustration. For short shots, work the ball against the wind so that you can control the ball and stop it quickly once it hits the green, though remember to take more club than you normally would for the same distance. On long shots you will not be able to fight the wind so use it to your advantage by starting off into the wind and letting it work round to safety.

Always swing just as normal, resisting the temptation to try to hit harder because of the wind. You will not hit it further by hitting harder. More likely you will lose control of the club head by snatching at the ball, resulting in a mis-timed shot.

From the fairway use your woods wherever possible, again playing the ball slightly further forward in your stance, adopting a square stance and swinging smoothly.

When you are close to the green you can use a headwind to help you control the ball. Play the ball centrally in your stance and hit

In cold weather make sure you have a warm jacket but one which does not restrict your movement too much. Rainproof trousers are vital if you are to feel comfortable and warm.

firmly, but smoothly, taking one more club than you normally need for the distance. I also prefer to stand slightly more open than I would on a short approach shot. The ball will rise into the wind and be held back by it, dropping almost vertically to stop without rolling forward.

Always use extra club into the wind rather than trying to hit harder.

Keeping dry on the course is vital. Use a good set of rainwear, waterproof shoes and an umbrella. Keep the clubs dry with a bag cover and carry extra gloves and a towel in the bag, to wipe the grips before you play a shot.

With a long shot downwind you should use something like a 3-wood to get the ball higher and take advantage of the wind, but on a shorter shot the wind will knock the ball down, so don't be afraid of hitting it high

Downwind

Downwind I would never use a driver off the tee, always favouring the 3-wood because it hits the ball higher, thus helping you to take even more advantage of the wind as well as controlling the direction better. Every little helps.

The same goes on the fairway where you should use one club less (or two depending on the strength of the wind) and hit it higher. When you reach the area around the green you might feel that hitting the ball high will just make it roll more on landing, and many players thus try to run the ball in low. That is fine if you have a flat approach with no problems to encounter but it does not allow

you to control the ball. A low bouncing ball is likely to roll more than one coming down at a steeper angle — obvious to any physics student but we so often forget these simple things.

You are, in fact, better advised to hit it high as you would for a normal approach shot, using one club less than normal. That will get the ball high with backspin and, on landing, it will stop.

This is one of those situations where you need to be brave to attempt the shot, but if you hit it with conviction rather than just patting at it you will find it works perfectly.

Cross winds are a bit of a problem but there are two basic

"rules" you need to learn.

On long shots, with a left-to-right wind, use the wind to fade the ball, aiming left to start with. On short shots with a left-to-right wind, draw the ball into the wind, fighting against it.

With a right-to-left wind, always hit into the wind, allowing the ball to be drawn round on the wind in the air. I am including a little illustration to make it easier to understand these "rules". Learn them and you will find playing in wind is less of a problem.

The wind can affect putts as well, so make a little allowance on the green if the wind is particularly strong.

In the wet your prime aim is to

The ball will be affected by a strong wind, even on a short pitch like this.

keep your hands and club grips dry. Carry extra towels and extra gloves, use a good rainproof suit, and dry your grips before you play each shot. Always remember to take at least one more club than you normally need for the distance, as wearing raingear — or something to keep warm in the winter, for that matter — restricts your shoulder turn. It's amazing how many golfers take a 5-iron for a shot of, say, 160 yards, summer or winter, wet or dry, wind or no wind.

Vary your shots to suit the conditions.

In the wet you will find it helpful to have some extra gloves in your golf bag and to wipe the grips before you play each shot

Perfect Bunker Shots

Earlier in this course we looked at how to play basic bunkers shots as well as how to cope with a plugged ball. We looked, too, at fairway bunkers. I want to move on now to the more awkward lies you might encounter in bunkers, particularly when the ball is on a slope in the sand; and also how to get the ball not just safely on the green but close to the pin, setting up either a birdie or, more likely, the opportunity to save par with a single putt.

It's worth reiterating briefly the main points about the basic bunker shot. The stance is normally slightly open, more open the closer you are to the pin; the club head must be aligned at the target, not left or right of it; the hands are pressed forward ahead of the ball, helping to cock the wrists early so that you do not have to worry about cocking them on the back swing; and you must swing the club back up to at least three-quarter length and follow through to a full finish. The swing should be fairly slow, but you must accelerate the club head into the sand an inch or so behind the ball, maintaining the club head speed as it bounces through impact, lifting the ball out on a cushion of sand.

The club should be lifted up fairly steeply and must be swung on the body and feet line, not the ball to target line. It is taken up almost vertically and will, in effect, be swinging outside the ball-to-target line.

A full follow-through from Alison Nicholas propels this ball high out of the bunker and safely onto the green.

The lower body remains fairly still throughout the shot, which is more of an arms and shoulders swing. Do try to keep the head still, by focusing one eye firmly on the back of the ball.

For a plugged lie a wedge might be more useful than the sand wedge; the stance should be rather more square. The aim here is to hit down just behind the back of the ball, leaving the club in the sand, almost like a punch shot. Although you must never quit on this shot you will find that your follow-through is restricted by the sand.

Practise bunker shots whenever you can, preferably from good, dry sand, though I will deal with wet sand a little later. I did also suggest that you practise bunker shots using an air ball, which will help you to understand that you must hit through fully if you are to get the ball out, rather than just stabbing at it.

Sloping Lies in Bunkers
Now for sloping lies in bunkers. Out on the fairway when you have a sloping lie you adjust your body line, judged by the shoulders, to parallel the slope. This is a natural reaction as you adjust your weight distribution automatically when you are standing on a slope.

In a bunker, on a downhill slope you do the same, setting your shoulders parallel to the slope. Most downhill bunker shots will be played from that awkward position at the rear of the bunker, often with the rear lip of the bunker interfering with the back swing. By aligning the shoulders level with the slope what you are

On a full bunker shot you need to take a fairly full swing, though at a slower pace than normal. Never be afraid of hitting right through the ball and finishing with the club held high

Practising with an air ball can help you to understand that you need to hit fairly hard

161

The club face always hits the ball at the same angle — the only thing that changes is the angle at which you are standing and thus swinging, and the angle of the slope

doing is to increase the steepness of the back swing, thus bringing the club up quickly, away from the sand and the rear lip of the bunker. You must, though, remember that if your club touches the sand you incur a penalty.

Think very carefully of what the club head must do. Ideally it has to be lifted away from the ball fairly steeply if it is to avoid the rear lip of the bunker. Then, on the way down it again has to miss the lip of the bunker, hit into the sand behind the ball at an unusually steep angle and then turn upwards, bouncing through the sand.

If you look at these two illustrations you will see that the ball trajectory, relative to the angle of the player, is the same in both cases. Yet because of the different angle of the player on the downslope the ball will not fly as high, and will run more on landing.

On a sloping fairway you adjust your shoulders to the terrain. Do the same in a bunker.

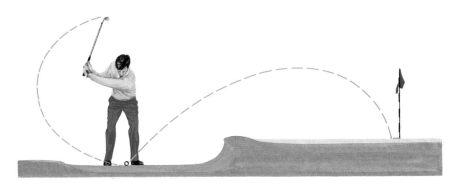

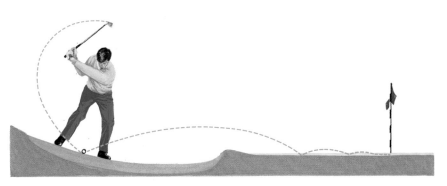

Because the arms and club are like a pendulum the swing arc is smooth, rather than the ideal shape as just described.

You can not change the shape of the arc — the laws of physics will not allow you to swing in an elliptical arc. All you can do is adjust to get the best contact you can in the sand behind and under the ball. You can see that this is not an easy shot.

Stand fairly open as the chances are you will have quite a lot of bunker to carry before you reach the green. You will find it very difficult to get much height on the ball off a downslope in a bunker. By standing open, with the club face aligned square to your target (which may be the fat of the green rather than the flag itself) you will increase the loft of the sand wedge, helping you to get the ball a little higher. Because you are open to the target the plane of the swing is sharply across the ball to target line. That will help you to get under the ball better, hitting it out higher. The higher it goes the softer it will land. That is the theory. However, because you have altered the angles by standing parallel to the slope, the ball will not have as much real height as you might expect. The illustration (left) shows this more clearly. The principle is the same for every sloping lie, uphill or downhill, and is worth understanding fully. It will make your golf that much easier.

The swing should be as slow as you dare, but at least three-quarters length, which, because of the angle at which you are standing, may seem much more, the club coming over the top to almost horizontal. Ensure you have enough club head speed coming down into the sand behind the ball. You must hit very hard even though you have a slow, smooth swing. Have the feeling that you are trying to hit a second ball one foot beyond the real ball, also down in the sand under the real ball. You need enough club head speed to hit that second ball cleanly. Your biggest problem is hitting hard enough to get the ball out of the bunker safely. Always choose a target where, if the ball rolls (which it will) you won't find yourself in another bunker!

With this shot it will be very difficult to stop the ball quickly. It is inevitable that it will roll some distance on landing so you normally have to be looking to get the ball to land on your side of the green. If the pin is cut close to your side of the green you have little real chance of leaving the ball stone dead. Your better option may be to get the ball onto the safety of the putting green and leave yourself with a long putt. It is at this stage of golf — when you are becoming an advanced player — that you begin to think more carefully about placing shots rather than just hitting them. This is a classic example of that type of situation.

Shots from the upslope of a bunker are much easier. Because of the placing of bunkers most shots which are caught in them hit the front of the bunker (the part closest to the green). A ball landing on a downslope has probably just rolled in (in which case it was short of its target) or has hit a bunker beyond the heart of the green (in which case it was too long). Those landing on an upslope have, in the main, just missed their target by the smallest of fractions, so don't

From a position at the back of a bunker you have to hit very hard to carry the bunker and get the ball safely on the green, though remember, it will run once it lands so ensure you are aiming at the fat of the green and not into more trouble

There is nothing to stop you from hitting out sideways or even backwards if that is the sensible thing to do

This little sequence shows that, from a three-quarter swing I am hitting down very hard and following through, throwing the weight at the shot as I come through the impact zone, and going on to a full finish. The ball stays very low but will reach the safety of the green, though I aimed it at the fat of the green rather than directly at the pin as it is impossible to stop the ball.

164

let the fact that you are in a bunker give you negative thoughts. Negative thoughts only lead to negative actions.

If you are on an upslope, take heart — you have a relatively easy shot. As always on a slope let nature dictate your stance, your shoulder line parallel to the slope. This will put your hands vertically above the ball, or very slightly behind it, rather than in front of it, though if you tilted the picture to horizontal you would see that your hands are, in effect, ahead of the ball, your weight more on your left

side. I must point out that it will not feel like that though, so do be careful and fully understand what I am saying. You can see by the photographs below that your stance never alters — only the level of the land alters.

You need to stand well open for this shot as the chances are you will need to get the ball up fairly quickly, possibly almost vertically, to clear the lip of the bunker.

Aim the club face directly at the target, get yourself a comfortable stance which will allow you to swing about three-quarters length

> Hitting the ball from the upslope of a bunker is relatively simple; all your need to do is to hit hard into the slope and the ball will rise and sit down once it lands on the green. The more open you stand the higher the ball will go, but the shorter will be the shot

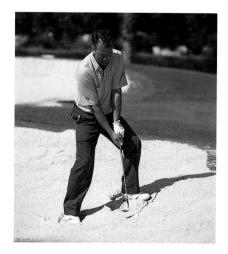

Above left On an upslope in a bunker do the same as on the fairway — adjust your shoulders to parallel the slope.

Above Get yourself comfortable before you attempt the shot as you must not lose your balance. . .

Left . . . and hit through slowly but fully, lifting the ball out on a cushion of sand.

In bunkers your main aim is to get yourself balanced to play the shot safely. Take your time and weigh up all the options before deciding to play the shot

without losing your balance, and hit fairly hard, following through as on any full shot.

This is a shoulders and arms swing, the lower body staying fairly still until after impact. Keep your head still, directly above the ball.

You will often find the ball plugged on an upslope, particularly when you have hit a short approach to the green, just missing it. This often happens on par-3 holes. Unlike the downslope, and every other shot from a sloping lie, on this occasion you do not adjust your balance to parallel the slope but to mirror it. You are, therefore, going against the slope. Think once again of the swing arc.

You must find a good stance, so that you remain balanced at least until impact. Hold the club with the blade almost horizontal and hit hard into the sand. You will have no possibility of a follow-through, the club just digging into the upslope, but do not attempt to cut off the follow-through — just let it happen.

With the ball on an upslope in a bunker, plugged or not, you have every opportunity of getting very close to the pin, unless it is on the other side of a wide or long green, or you are trying to go up a sloping green. The aim is to hit hard into the sand just below the ball, literally blasting it upwards on a cushion of sand. The steeper the slope the more vertically the ball will rise; the more vertically it rises the shorter it will roll on landing.

If the pin is close to your side of the green you have every possibility of landing it very close, but if it is some way away you might need to try to push the ball forward more, by altering the angle of attack of the club head into the

sand, but I must add that much depends on how close to the edge of the bunker you are, and how high the lip of the bunker is. With an overhanging lip your only choice is to blast the ball out high and hope it kicks forward as it lands. Do make sure that there is enough loft on the club to clear the lip of the bunker. The ball will only come out if there is enough room for it to do so.

There is something you can do to make it roll forward if you have some green to cover, and this is to close the club face a little, but again, make sure you still have enough loft on the club to get the ball over the lip of the bunker and safely onto the green. On the other hand if you want the ball to go straight up and down, to a pin cut very close, open the face of the club more so that you get more loft on the shot. I would emphasise that in both cases you still have the club face square to the target and open or close it by adjusting your feet and body line; you do not aim the club face left or right of the target. This point is very important and often catches out the less experienced golfer, with obvious results. It is vital you understand it, for bunker shots as well as for any others.

Possibly the biggest problem with sloping bunker shots is finding a secure position in which to stand. Often you will have to stand in a very difficult position, perhaps with only one foot in the bunker. In these circumstances the

With a lip to the bunker Faldo has no option but to blast the ball out high, but with very little follow-through possible. The club face must be almost horizontal as it hits into the sand beneath the ball.

166

professionals really come into their own, often taking quite a long time to get the right balance and to make sure that they can swing their arms effectively without losing their balance. Watch them carefully at any golf tournament and you will see just how long they take getting their balance before attempting the shot. Take as much time as you need; you only have one chance.

Side lies, with the ball either above or below your feet in the sand should be tackled just as you would a shot on the fairway, adjusting your posture to compensate for the ball position.

With the ball above your feet you should grip further down the club and remember to compensate for the fact that the ball will hook left. As the club has in effect been raised in front of you the face has closed — remember our experiment with a tee-peg stuck to the face of the club in the first part of this course. You may have to compensate by aiming the club face more to the right of the target and you will also have to open the face a little so that you do not hit the ball downwards but up. This is one of the only times I would not aim the club face at the target. Be very careful on this shot, swinging slowly though never quitting on the shot. Practise this one in your practice bunker — although this situation is rare on the course you should be prepared for all eventualities.

With a ball in the sand below your feet the opposite happens — the face is relatively more open and the ball is likely to slice a little to the right. You might, therefore, need to play the ball further back in your stance and aim it further left, though you must never close or hood the club face.

168

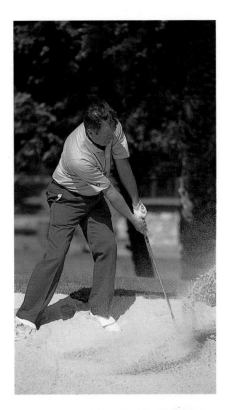

Top row With a three-quarter swing I try to keep my head still above the ball but hit through slowly, lifting the ball out fairly gently.

Far left You can see how, with the ball below my feet, I am standing well open but with the ball back in the stance. I am trying to keep my spine as straight as possible and the club face is aiming left of the flag to compensate for the effective open shape of the club face, something I have dealt with earlier.

Left With the ball above your feet you need to grip down, open your stance and hit through, splashing the ball out. Because the ball will follow the slope you again need to aim it to the right slightly, in effect cutting under the ball. You can clearly see that I have done this by the position of the club at impact. This causes the ball to stop better once it hits the green.

169

Wet sand stops the sand wedge bounding through the sand under the ball as it should, so you might need to hit down harder or use a wedge which will dig in a little more, rather than thinning the ball

Wet Sand

Although it is no fun playing golf in the rain many people have precious little opportunity of getting out to play golf, so a spot of rain (!) will hardly deter them. It often happens, particularly in the winter months, that we need to play out of bunkers where the sand is wet.

Indeed, many bunkers are flooded in the winter months. The rules of golf allow you to lift a ball from casual water in a bunker or to move the ball if it means having to stand in water to play your shot. You do, however, still have to drop the ball in another part of the bunker, no closer to the hole. Sometimes not even this is possible and, if I am playing a friendly round of golf I would ask my playing partners if they minded if I dropped the ball outside the bunker. I won't tell you which ones refuse!

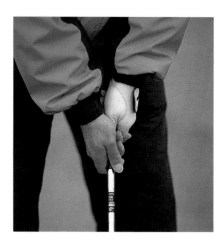

In wet sand grip right down the club. If you do not have to hit the shot too far you might find it helps to weaken your left hand grip, but keep the right hand in its normal position.

You must hit fairly hard, though, in wet sand or the ball will not come out. Whatever you do, don't thin the ball. Hit under it into the sand.

If it is possible to play the ball from within the confines of a wet bunker, you need to discover just how hard and compacted the sand is. I am going to assume that it is pretty wet.

By shuffling your feet about in the bunker you can tell just how compacted the sand is. If it is really hard the sand wedge might not be the best club as it would just bounce. Considering an ordinary wedge instead.

You can still control the ball on this shot if you play it carefully. Grip the club as low as you possibly can, your right hand at the very bottom of the grip. Stand very open to the target, though you must aim the club face at the target itself. Because of your stance the club face is almost horizontal.

The swing needs to be rather wristy, really working the hands through impact. The arms tend to do little work.

As you swing back, probably no more than waist high, your wrists cock early and sharply, increasing the width of the swing arc, though your arms are nowhere near as far back. As you come through impact your hands do all the work, bringing the club head through the ball very quickly, which is why it is so important to grip right down.

The follow-through varies, according to the length of the shot. For a long shot you can continue through as normal, though this will not allow you to control the ball. It will probably fly 20 yards, so only do this if you have sufficient green to work with.

If the pin is fairly close you need to not only cut off the follow-through but to pull the hands sharply round to the left of the body immediately after impact.

This, in effect, means you are hitting a really strong out-to-in shot across the ball, cutting it very severely.

In both cases the back of the left hand finishes pointing skywards, the club face also coming out in that horizontal position it had at address. One professional I have worked with, Ron Pettit at the Royal Sydney Golf Club, used to say that you should have sand sitting on the club face at the finish.

You can see that these specialist shots are ones you need to master in the practice bunker before trying them out on the course. Learn them now — play them later.

With a wet, flat bunker and no lip to go over the best option might

Putting from sand when there is no lip and the sand is firm is easy. Hit the ball on its equator, but firmly and it will hop, skip and jump onto the green perfectly. It is a shot very few golfers know, but terribly easy and highly effective. If you have a flat bunker, try it, wet or dry.

To cut off a bunker shot finish with the back of your left hand, and the club face, pointing to the sky. You should have the feeling that you could balance some sand on it at the finish

There is nothing to stop you from putting from wet sand if the bunker is flat enough. Hit the ball on the equator and make sure you follow through fully, the putter aiming at the target as you finish

171

The best hour you could spend would be in having a bunker lesson from your club professional — it will do you far more good than standing at the driving range hitting golf balls into the distance

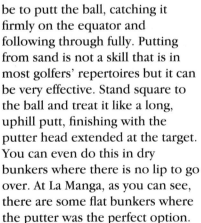

be to putt the ball, catching it firmly on the equator and following through fully. Putting from sand is not a skill that is in most golfers' repertoires but it can be very effective. Stand square to the ball and treat it like a long, uphill putt, finishing with the putter head extended at the target. You can even do this in dry bunkers where there is no lip to go over. At La Manga, as you can see, there are some flat bunkers where the putter was the perfect option.

Opposite Just to reiterate the point I made in the first part of this course about long bunker shots using a 5-wood. Address the ball in the middle to centre of your stance, don't over-swing and pick the ball off the sand cleanly, as you should off the fairway with this club. There is no real divot of sand and the ball will fly long and true.

Above With about 100 yard to go I would use an 8-iron, gripping well down. Stand slightly open and take a three-quarters swing, then hit through taking very little sand. The ball will come out strong but because of your stance will slice nicely and land on the back of the green. Obviously you start it to the left of the green to bring it back.

Steep Bunkers
If you are up against the face of a very steep bunker with an over-hanging lip which will make it difficult to hit the ball forward very far, you may not have enough loft on the sand wedge to get the ball out of the sand. In that case your only option is to play out sideways or even backwards, taking very great care to find a safe landing spot first.

To quickly test whether you have enough loft on the club, hold the blade as open as you can, the face being as horizontal as it would be if you were swinging it into the sand behind the ball. If the angle of the club face is less than the face of the bunker the ball, quite simply, will not come out. You can't defeat nature.

If you do have enough loft on the club face, stand as open as you can to help get the club face almost horizontal, though with the face aiming at the target. Swing slowly and hit hard, not attempting to quit on the shot, though chances are the club will stop as it hits into the bunker face.

Short Bunker Shots
Stopping the ball from a bunker shot when the pin is cut very close to the edge of the bunker is a problem for most higher handicap golfers, but for better players and professionals, it is fairly simple.

Basically the ball needs to be hit higher to land softly, and with as much backspin as possible.

I try to play such a shot a little further forward in my stance than normal, though do remember that you position the ball in your square stance first, then open the line of your feet.

The ball needs to be played with the face held close to horizontal, which you do by aiming the club face at the target and then opening your stance. The shot is rather more wristy than normal, though do swing back to about three-quarters. It needs a steep take-away and a sharp cut across the ball to get it out safely.

As you come through the impact zone the hands have to work overtime, almost as they would when playing squash. The ball will then float out.

You might need to cut the shot

off but you don't do that by quitting on the shot but by holding the follow-through, the back of the left hand finishing facing the sky and your arms not reaching more than about shoulder height going through. Once again, as with the short shot from wet sand, you can cut the shot off well left of the body.

Fairway Bunkers
I suggested earlier in this course that fairway bunkers were fairly easy to get out of, by catching the ball cleanly as it sits on the top of the sand. In many cases you have little hope of reaching the green, the aim being to get out onto the fairway in an ideal position for the next shot.

There are occasions, though, when you find a bunker about 100 yards from the green, especially on a long par-5 or short par-4, in which case you should be looking to land the ball safely on the green.

The first thing to look at is the distance, then take one or two clubs more than is necessary. I would favour two clubs extra, with the intention of landing on the back of the green, which is normally softer (not so many people hit past the flag so they don't tread the grass down as much as at the front), allowing me to control the ball as it lands.

An interesting sequence as I hit the ball from a bunker with a steep mound to get over. Stand fairly open and swing slowly, getting right under the ball as you can see from the lower picture where the ball is already airborne on a cushion of sand. The hands do not allow the club to go right through straight away, holding it back slightly to control the distance.

From a fairway bunker the more experienced golfer could use a 5-wood; make sure you take the ball off the sand cleanly, though it might fade a little

For a shot of 100 yards, then, which is within range of a wedge normally, I would take an 8-iron. Grip down halfway, open your stance, with the club face aiming at the target, which might not be the pin itself if the fat part of the green is safer. This set up means you will slice the ball. Take a full swing and hit hard and right through the ball. You will slice the ball onto the green, helping it to stop quickly on landing. A sliced shot goes less distance than one hit straight, so you can see why it is necessary to take extra club.

I believe this is one of Greg Norman's favourite shots.

I hope this has given you a better understanding of how to play bunker shots. I have to say that I find them fascinating — but then I have a warped sense of humour! —

On a short bunker shot where I want the ball to stop quickly I pull my hands sharply left round my body, keeping the club face pointing to the sky. You must, though, hit through the impact zone, never quitting on the shot.

because they allow you to be so inventive and to learn so much about how to use the golf club.

What I have shown you here is what works for me and I am fortunate enough to have seen hundreds of the best golfers in the world playing from bunkers, not just on the golf course but in the practice bunker.

Fred Couples holds the follow-through on this short bunker shot.

The best hour you could spend is in having a sand lesson from your local golf professional. I guarantee you will find it of more value than a lesson on driving, but before doing this, become a competent straightforward sand player first. The less experienced golfer is frightened of sand but if you approach a bunker shot positively, having built that confidence through regular practice, you will gain the greatest satisfaction from playing a shot from an "impossible" situation to within inches of the pin. It devastates your opponents.

Single Putting

In the earlier part of this course we dealt with straightforward putts on a flat green. As you know only too well, not all putts are quite that simple, and on sloping greens you must acquire the ability to "read" the greens, deciding, literally on the spot, how far to one side of the hole you must hit the shot, and with what strength, to get the ball into the hole.

I have already dealt with how important putting is if you want to lower your scores. You are allowed 36 putts per round by the par of each course, two per green. Good players are looking to play around 32 putts per round at maximum. How many did you take on your last round?

At La Manga, where we took most of the photographs for this book, I kept a little secondary "scorecard" just detailing my putting. You can do the same if you really want to improve this part of your game.

Use the sample card on this page or write to me for a special card you can use on the course, then send it back to me for a personal analysis.

The point about putting is that you are, with very few exceptions, trying to get the ball into the hole. Be aggressive on the greens, forget about lagging the ball up short. Get the ball **in** the hole!

1992 US Masters champion Fred Couples has an unusual putting stroke in that he "stabs" at the ball rather than stroking it, yet his technique works for him and this is an important lesson for all golfers, particularly as putting is such an individual skill.

On flat greens, as we saw earlier, you aim the putter head straight and swing it using a pendulum motion through the ball, the wrists staying firm and the putter head finishing extending towards the hole.

I would refine this a little now that we are moving onto more advanced techniques by telling you to extend the right hand through to the target. To do this you must

Hole	1st putt Distance	1st putt Direction	2nd putt Distance	2nd putt Direction	3rd putt Distance	3rd putt Direction
1	✓	L	✓	✓		
2	T	L	✓	✓		
3	✓	✓	——			
4	S	R	✓	✓		
5	S	✓	✓	✓		
6	✓	L	✓	✓		
7	S	✓	✓	✓		
8	T	L	✓	L	✓	✓
9	S	L	✓	✓		

Key:

Distance: S = Short; T = Long; √ = On-target
Direction L = Left;   R = Right; √ = On-target

Use this card on your course to check your putting expertise. Write to me for some sample cards and details of a putting analysis service.

Do you know how many putts you took during your last round of golf? Use this putting chart to help you, and to show you where you are going wrong on the greens

This is my putting chart for the first nine holes at La Manga. You can see that I have taken eighteen putts, which is "par", yet I have a few areas to improve on. In the first column I have noted the distance and direction of my first putts, leaving four short, being long on two and about the correct distance on the other three. I have also pulled too many putts to the left, five of them staying that side, with three on-target and one drifting right.

When you have a very short putt extend the putter head across the hole itself — that helps you sink more putts

Avoid the temptation to take the putter straight back as that will force it outside the line; your need to take it back very slightly inside

Although you may stand with your feet line very slightly open to the target you should have your shoulders parallel to the target line

check your putting grip to ensure that your right palm is facing the target at address. It must finish pointing at the target too, with the wrist still being firmly locked rather than cupped or arched. Don't roll it as you do with a normal golf shot — putting has little to do with normal golf. The right hand controls the putt and you need to get the feeling that it is the right hand alone which is directing the putt. I would suggest that you practise putting just with your right hand if you really want to be a good putter.

The other point which is of vital importance is to follow through after you have hit the ball, particularly on a short putt when you should finish with the putter head almost over the hole itself. On a longer putt the putter head, and back of your left hand are extended at the hole (or target on a sloping green) as you finish.

I also find it helpful, particularly on long putts where you want the ball to stay on line and run on, to take the putter back inside the ball-to-target line, rather than trying to keep it straight as some golf teachers suggest. I always feel that if you try to keep it too straight going back you will, in fact, be pushing it outside the line thus bringing the putter across the ball from out-to-in as you hit the ball, causing a mis-hit.

We have to acknowledge that not all greens are as flat as a billiard table, so you have to carefully estimate the amount of borrow you need and the speed of the green. Don't worry too much about the grain of the green at the moment as that is introducing a further distraction.

Finding the speed of the greens

To attack the hole you need to extend the right hand and putter head through towards the hole as this photograph clearly shows. Although purists might note that my right palm is not aiming directly at the hole, with the camera angle and the fact that I have allowed for the borrow, the ball will (and did!) finish very close.

is best done on the practice green before you begin your round. Using some of the practice routines at the end of the section on putting in the first part of this course try to hit putts from different angles, both uphill, downhill and across the slope.

You will generally find that a green more exposed to the wind is faster than one which may be sheltered as it has more opportunity to dry out. A large shadow on a green, cast by a tree, perhaps, will slow the green a little. The speed also varies according to the time of day, most greens being slightly damp in the morning and thus slower. By the end of the day they will have been trodden down by many golfers and the ground may be thus a little more compacted. A worse problem when playing a green late in the day is that the greens, particularly close to the hole itself, will have become spiked by the many pairs of golf shoes walking across it. The surface might be a little uneven at that time of day so look very carefully at your line.

In such circumstances, when there are spike marks clearly visible, watch your partners' putts carefully to see if they bobble rather than rolling flat. If they do, hit the ball more square on, the putter head almost resting on the ground. You are, in effect, hitting the ball lower down which will give it a more solid strike and keep it on line better on that surface.

In summer the greens, unless constantly watered, may tend to "seed" a little, making them faster. Then, you want to hit the ball on its equator.

A wet green is always slower so if you are playing in wet or humid conditions, be aware that you will have to hit harder, particularly going uphill.

You will get to know the greens on your own course quite well after a few rounds, but on a course you don't know, the art of successful putting is to learn quickly from your putts as well as those of your playing partners. Watch theirs carefully, seeing if they hit putts hard or very gently, and then where the ball finishes. Watch the ball particularly when it is close to the hole, to see if it is thrown off-line by any little irregularity in the surface.

Although you only use the putter on the green — or very close to it — you do need to have some idea of where you want to land the ball on your approach shot to give you the best possible position from which to putt.

It is always better to have an uphill putt if possible, and on two-tier greens you need to get your ball on the same level as the pin to stand a good chance of sinking the first putt. If the pin is on the lower level the worst place you could possibly be is on the upper level. You would almost be better leaving the approach short and having a chip up to the green, if it is slightly elevated.

When you reach the green always walk round the putt rather than just looking at it from one angle. What appears to be a gentle left to right slope might turn out to be rather different when looked at from another angle. Look also for double breaks, which are quite common and where the ball would move one way first before turning again as it reaches the second gradient. To see gradients best get as low as you can so your eyes can see the contours of the green. Don't rush this. Be certain of your line. Take your time.

You will often see professionals "plumb-bobbing" — holding the putter in front of them to try to estimate how much of a slope they need to compensate for in hitting their putt.

Do this by holding the putter in front of you with the shaft obscuring the ball and covering the hole itself. On a sloping green you will be able to see more of the hole either left or right of the shaft. If more of the hole can be seen on the left side of the shaft the green slopes to the left, so you need to hit it to the right to compensate; if more of the hole appears on the

A wet green, or one that is in the shadow of the trees, will normally be a little slower than one exposed to the wind or in direct sunlight

Walk round the green a little before you putt as this will give you a better idea of any slopes

Plumb bobbing is a good way to see any tiny slopes near the hole itself but trust your eyes as you approach the green — the green often slopes the same way as the ground around it

right the opposite is true. The more severe the slope the more of the hole you will be able to see on one side.

On sloping greens too, the faster the surface the further up the slope you need to aim if the ball is to come round properly.

All professionals use plumb-bobbing to check the slope of the green. I have explained it in the text and it can help you, particularly when no break is evident at first glance. Very few greens are absolutely flat.

A putt up over a ridge will also often involve a slope so pay careful attention to the exact contours. This putt, uphill and across a slope, seems to be going left of the pin (right from this angle), yet there is an interesting double break which brought the ball back to within three inches. You need to take as much time as professionals over putts if you really want to cut your scores, despite the constant calls to speed up golf. That can be done in other ways. On the green be absolutely certain of your line. Take your time!

It is, sadly, not something I can teach you — only practice and patience will do that. I can, however, make you aware of the principles involved.

Another desperately difficult putt, particularly on a fast green, is the downhill putt. On some greens, if you miss a short downhill putt you could face an even longer one coming back uphill. Eamon Darcy, the great Irish golfer, has said that on a very fast downhill putt on one course, Golf del Sur, in Tenerife, he hit the ball merely "with the shadow of the putter". Some of them have to be this delicate.

One way to stop a downhill putt is to strike the ball more with the toe of the putter than the sweet spot. You are, in effect, putting side spin on the ball, just as when you slice a shot. As we have seen, a sliced ball will travel less distance, pulling up quickly on landing.

Because the ball is spinning clockwise if sliced — even with a putter — it will tend to stop quicker, rather than rolling on and on.

You must aim correctly, but just bring the putter head across the ball from out to in. Be very careful that you do not close the face as you try to hit it more towards the toe. It is still a stroke from the shoulders rather than an over-use of the hands. You also have to bring the putter round the body more to the left on the follow-through, rather than aiming it straight at the hole. This is a very delicate shot and I will take you through it one more time.

Set up a little more open than normal, the ball addressed off the toe of the club. Swing the putter very gently on the body line, so that it goes well outside the ball to

On a fast downhill putt you can stop the ball by addressing it off the toe of the putter and then by pulling the putter head across the ball as you hit it, rather like a bunker shot or any other shot you wish to slice

It is always best to have an uphill putt so take your time and look around to see where you want to leave the ball if you have little chance of holing it first time

Always look for a midway point on the green if you have a slope or double break to contend with

target line. Then, just before you strike the ball, snap the putter sharply left, round your body. The entire stroke is very delicate; never hit the ball too hard, but do give it enough power to roll towards the hole. The fact that it is rolling with slice spin will stop it quickly.

Try it on very fast downhill putts; you will see that it works.

It is appropriate here to say that if you want a ball to roll very straight you need to hit it with topspin, catching it on the equator, the putter head off the ground as it reaches the impact zone. I have explained that more fully, though, in the first part of this course.

I want to deal now with putts where you need to be aggressive, though within reason. Uphill putts are the best you can have, even if the green also slopes from left to right or vice-versa. On these the ball should be struck with the sweet spot of the putter, the right hand following through, extending the putter head at the target. Do be careful not to break the wrist set as you swing back, or as you follow through. At the finish I want to see the same unbroken line we had at address. The 45 back/55 through ratio still applies so restrict your back swing. That will, or should, resist any temptation to hinge the wrists.

Although you don't want to end past the hole, leaving you with a downhill putt, you do need to be aggressive enough to get the ball into the hole. Only in certain circumstances, where you need to defend a lead on your opponent for example, should you be thinking of lagging the putt and then only to within six inches. It is a serious waste of a shot to leave

an uphill putt more than a foot away from the hole.

Some uphill putts are also downhill putts, when, for example, the green has a ridge that you have to putt up and over before reaching the hole. In these cases you need to give the ball just enough power to get over the top of the ridge, then letting it roll under its own momentum downhill. These are difficult putts and again it is only through practice that you will acquire the experience necessary to play them well.

A good idea on these putts is to have a midway point between you and the hole from where the ball should roll fairly straight to the hole. You should then be looking to putt to that midway point so that the ball will end in or close to the hole. It's the same as looking for a midway target on the fairway when shaping a shot.

To stop a ball on a fast downhill putt try addressing it off the toe of the putter rather than the sweet spot. You can clearly see, from the white mark on the putter showing the sweet spot, how far towards the toe I have addressed this.

Another little trick is to pull the putter round to your left after striking it. In effect this is hitting the ball a glancing blow, just enough to get the ball rolling. There is no follow-through as on a normal putt.

185

You sometimes find a green with the opposite problem, there being a dip between the ball and the hole. Here you need to putt downhill first, hitting the ball sufficiently strongly that it will climb the upslope. You ought to be aggressive on such putts as, if you fail to reach the hole, you could find the ball rolling back down to finish in the valley.

On a sloping green choose a midway point to calculate how the ball will roll; remember it will turn more as it slows down towards the end of a putt. And no, I did not leave the flag in to putt — the photograph just looks better with the extra colours!

There are many occasions, particularly when the ground is hard and flat, when you can putt from well off the green. Do check very carefully that the grass between you and the green itself has no little clumps or bumps that might either throw the ball off line or slow it down. Unless you have a smooth, hard approach area to the green and the flag is not too far on the green, the more experienced player really is best advised to chip with a short iron, particularly if using a balata ball. If, however, that part of your game lacks a little confidence, use the putter. Just make sure you can strike the ball with sufficient pace to get it on the green and close to the hole.

Another problem you will encounter from time to time is when the ball is sitting against the fringe of the green, the longer grass preventing you from getting the putter head smoothly into the back of the ball.

Here you have two options and they depend very much on the length of the putt. As normally the pin is not cut too close to the edge of the green, the chances are that you will be facing a reasonable putting distance, more than 20 feet. My advice here is to use a wedge and "blade" the shot, in effect thinning it by hitting exactly on the equator of the ball with a very "open" club face. I must explain that by "open" at this stage I mean that the blade is not pointing right of the target but is held in such a way that the face is virtually horizontal but facing the target, taking any borrow into account.

There is a terrible amount of confusion on this subject, and it is one I have mentioned more than once in this series, but I do feel it needs constantly emphasising. The ball goes where it is aimed, so always aim the club face at the target. Any adjustments you make are to the body line, which affects the plane of the swing. Always aim the club face at the target.

By blading this shot you will skim the ball across the surface of the green. Your other option, which I might prefer if the hole is closer to me, is to hit a descending blow with the putter, treating it almost as an iron shot, hitting down and through the ball rather than stroking it as I would a normal putt. You must be very careful not to close the putter face at impact though, and be sure to follow through, extending the putter head at the target.

Set up to this shot as if you were on a downslope, your shoulders parallel to that imaginary slope, pushing your hands well ahead of the ball. Don't swing back too far but do try to have the feeling that you are putting downhill on the fairway.

With a ball against the fringe the best option is to hit down with the putter, but follow through if you have a long putt as hitting down on the ball will bounce it slightly and put backspin on it, causing it to stop fairly quickly.

From a situation where the ball is up against the fringe on the edge of the green you have two options: either use the putter, hitting down into the back of the ball or use the wedge, "blading" the ball, catching it right on its equator with the leading edge of the club; that will send it rolling across the green. You can afford to be fairly aggressive with these shots as the ball will stop fairly quickly if you catch it perfectly

Equipment

I am very grateful to Bill Reid, Golf Director of Wisley Golf Club in Surrey, and to Philip Morley, Managing Director of MacGregor Golf, UK, who also supplied the clubs used in our photographs, for their enormous help in putting together this section of our course. Their experience over many years of matching clubs to players has produced major benefits, for without the right equipment you will only be half a golfer.

Having correctly matched equipment to suit your game is essential, at whatever level you play. The newcomer to golf may well find the game improver clubs — peripherally weighted, cavity-back clubs — ideal, as they help to counteract any minor inconsistencies in the swing. Of course they won't make a bad swing good but they do have a positive effect as their extra head weight promotes a better downward strike into the back of the ball, resulting in a cleaner contact on a larger 'sweet spot' with the ball getting airborne faster and spinning better.

There is nothing wrong with players of any standard using this type of club; many professionals on both the European and US Tours use them and I would strongly recommend this type of club for virtually every lady golfer, for senior golfers and for the majority of average players.

Those who play to a higher standard may find it beneficial to use a more traditional shape of club, known as a blade. Most cavity backed clubs are cast; blades tend to be forged and are thus of softer

material, giving greater "feel" to the advanced golfer, particularly in the shorter clubs. Many professionals who use cavity-back clubs from the 2-iron to about the 8- or 9-iron will complement their set by including a couple of extra wedges, normally blades, because there is a genuine need for extra "feel" in those short irons. Despite the excellence of many of today's cavity-back clubs a blade still does have advantages round the green and, in my opinion, out of sand.

What clubs should you buy, therefore, and what should you be looking for in that set of clubs?

First you need to decide whether the peripherally-weighted clubs or blades suit you best. Overall, anyone with a handicap of about 9 or more should opt for peripherally-weighted clubs, though it comes down to personal choice. Before you choose I would suggest that you borrow something like a 5-iron and a shorter club (9-iron) of each type to see which you find most comfortable and even then take a couple of different models. You will immediately notice that the shot with a blade will fly lower, not rising as much as a cavity-backed club.

You then need to find the correct length of the club. This is more important than you might think, because clubs come in standard lengths, a normal 5-iron having a shaft length. This has not changed in 50 years, yet we know from other data that people now grow taller than they did 50 years ago, on average.

That suggests that clubs should also be a little longer than they

Getting the right clubs for your game is as important as buying the correct pair of shoes. Try various clubs before you buy — they are not cheap

Cavity-backed clubs normally hit the ball higher, giving you better control once it lands

were then. Bill Reid believes that just a half inch extra in the length of a club would produce a better swing, for taller players at least. It is easy to understand why.

You could try this with a cut-down club if you can get hold of one, or just look at the difference between the swing pattern for the driver and the wedge. With a very short club the swing is much more upright as the club is held, at address, closer to the body. This reduces the length of the swing arc, and it becomes impossible to get as much club head speed at impact as with a longer club, which is why the driver hits the ball further than the wedge (or should do!). As a result less power is produced at impact. A very upright swing also prevents the hips from turning out of the way on the downswing, possibly causing an out-to-in shot, the club face coming across the ball from right to left, producing either a slice or a straight pull left. This is just one reason why you should stand slightly open when using the shorter clubs.

It is very easy to have a half inch added to your clubs, whether steel or graphite, and most professionals, having sold you a set of clubs, would carry out this alteration either free of charge or for a nominal amount. Either way you will gain more in results on the golf course than it has cost. Do have your golf professional check your height and swing pattern, particularly if you are a taller than average player, though the majority of golfers will find their clubs are ideal.

Conversely, for shorter players — I believe the politically correct term is now vertically disadvantaged! — the standard clubs may be too long, producing an overly flat swing. Clubs can be cut down very easily.

Although most people, when buying clubs, worry about the lie of the club the length is probably just as important. If the length is correct the lie may be correct and would not need altering. Golf shafts come today in five different degrees of flex, or thickness. I have

> You can have the length of your clubs altered to suit you as well as having the correct size grips fitted. Have your clubs regripped regularly and also have the loft and lie checked as they tend to get knocked out of position, particularly on hard fairways in the summer

> If you have graphite shafts you should have a golf bag with soft dividers as this will protect the shafts and prevent 'ringing'. You can also use some masking tape to cover the shafts where they touch the rim of the bag; this adds to their protection

CORRECT SHAFT FLEX			
Type of shaft	Typical golfer	Driver distance (yards)	5-iron distance (yards)
X – extra stiff	top professional	250+	185+
S – stiff	good professional, top amateur and single figure golfers	215-250	160-185
R – regular	average man, low handicap woman	175-225	130-170
A – flexible	senior golfers, men and women	150-185	110-140
L – ladies	average woman golfer	less than 160	less than 115

Stiffer shafts are normally ideal for better players and for those with very fast swings. Other players should have more flexible shafts but ask your club professional to check your swing speed so that you can get the best out of your game

included a little chart based on the yardage achieved with a 5-iron and driver which illustrates which type of shaft each player should use. Whilst Tour professionals use extra stiff shafts, only the very best amateur players should use the same, stiff being ideal for better players. Average golfers should stay with regular shafts until they improve to the point where stiff shafts, which do give extra distance and direction, could be of benefit.

Some graphite shafts are classified as 'firm' rather than stiff so check with your golf professional or with the manufacturer's specifications. Your golf professional is the best qualified to advise you.

Ladies' shafts come in two thicknesses, for average and for stronger players. Some senior men golfers will find the ladies' stronger clubs could be of major benefit.

Hitting a club with a shaft that is too stiff for your particular swing will almost invariably lead to a slice or a push right (left for left-handers). Most clubs you buy are fitted with regular shafts, but you can easily have them changed by your club professional.

The MacGregor reverse draft clubs I have used in this course are manufactured using an extension of the peripheral weighting which most cavity-back clubs have. MacGregor RD clubs have a larger sweet spot and a better distribution of weight in the toe of the club. From a golfer's point of view they are a joy to play with, and I tried many different clubs before deciding on these. The shafts are lighter than normal but are firmer than regular shafts adding distance as well as accuracy.

The woods, too, feature a similar principle though I chose the Jumbo driver, primarily because I had not used one before and it felt good. I am certain that, as in tennis racquet design a few years back, mid-size and jumbo size golf clubs are the way forward for many manufacturers. Do try them before you buy, though, however good they look.

A further point to choose carefully is the grip. Grips come in a variety of styles and sizes. For higher handicap players there are now grips which have a dimple effect rather than the traditional cord surface. These can lead to a better "feel" in the hands; that should lead to better golf.

Getting the right grip size is vital. As you grip the club the middle two fingers of the left hand should just about touch the thumb pad. If they do not touch, get smaller grips fitted; if they overlap too much have larger grips fitted, even up to extra large size, which are also ideal for people who may have arthritic hands or fingers, particularly as they grow older.

Grip size really is important — you buy golf gloves to fit your hands, so get grips to fit them also. If the grip is too small your hands are squeezed tighter on the grip, creating more hand and forearm pressure which leads to less feel in the shot and thus less control.

Graphite shafts tend to be thinner than steel, so the grips are normally thinner as well. Again, check your size carefully and have larger grips fitted if necessary.

It is important that your grips be kept clean and in first-class condition, though sadly many golfers let themselves down in this respect.

The Lie of a Golf Club

A golf club must have the correct lie for your height and swing pattern if you are to get the best from it. Before you buy a set of golf clubs ask your professional to check the lie carefully for you. Even with modern manufacturing methods you may find one club in a set has a slightly different lie to the rest, so ask him to check them all.

Basically, if you are tall, you need your clubs to be more upright; if you are shorter they should be flatter. The diagram below shows this. With a club too flat you will risk hitting the ground with the toe first, causing the club face to swing out, slicing the ball.

With clubs too upright the opposite happens, the heel of the club hitting the ground first, causing a hook.

To avoid either of these, get your clubs checked and have them rechecked at least every year because they do get knocked out of position sometimes, particularly during the summer when you may be playing on hard fairways.

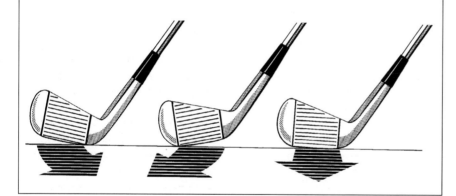

Playing with worn grips, or shiny gloves is like driving a car with bald tyres — you get no grip

After every few games, summer or winter, you should scrub the grips with a soft nail brush and warm, soapy water. This removes any dirt, grease or perspiration from the grips and leaves them actually feeling cleaner. That will allow you to grip them better and play better. Leave them to dry in an airy room, not a dark cupboard.

They should be regripped regularly, at least once a year. Playing with worn grips is like driving a car on bald tyres. You get no control and, although you may not perceive it, the club will twist in your hands during the swing, leading to wayward shots. Tour players regrip probably about every month or so, but they do use their clubs every day. For the average player it is not necessary to have them changed that often, but once they do begin to feel a little shiny, get them changed. You don't have to have the complete set regripped as you will find you use some clubs more often than others.

Gloves too, need changing regularly. The all-weather gloves are probably ideal for the average golfer as they can be washed gently in warm water. They will, though, wear out and if you play with worn gloves you will be adding three or four strokes to every round.

The incorrect lie on your golf clubs will affect your swing, either causing your to slice or hook the ball. Get them checked

Although you might not have a caddy to do it for you, you should wipe grass from the club face before, and after every shot. Grass between the club face and ball prevents the ball from spinning correctly and will lead to poorly controlled shots

Many golfers wear their gloves out on the heel of the hand, opposite the base of the thumb. This is caused either by a poor grip technique — so ask your professional to check your grip for you — or because the grips are the wrong size as I have outlined above.

For better players who want extra "feel" in their hands, leather gloves are an option, but not an inexpensive one.

Keep your golf clubs clean and dry at all times. I carry a nail brush in my bag at all times to clean the grooves. Getting rid of any dirt or grass from the grooves is essential if you want to hit clean golf shots.

Many players go round the course with their club faces dirty. This will result in missed shots as any grass between the club face and ball stops the club face from doing its job of controlling the ball.

Even after a couple of practice swings, out on the course, you should wipe any grass from the club face — most professionals wipe the club on their trousers — before playing the shot.

And finally, golf balls. Professionals use balata, normally with a pressure rating of 100. Balata balls have a softer covering which allows the ball to be controlled more readily, though they do split

quite easily, most professionals changing their ball about every fourth hole in a tournament. Whilst better players (less than 12 handicap) would benefit from balata, possibly with 90 compression, the average player will find the surlyn balls with a 90 compression are ideal for him. Ladies have a choice of balls with a compression of 80 and these are also ideal for average men on very cold winter days. The weather does affect a golf ball quite considerably. A shot of 200 yards on a warm summer's day would only travel 185 yards on a winter's morning when the temperature is still hovering around zero. Humidity also affects the ball, making it feel heavier and so losing distance. The same happens in rain. Remember these things when you are playing and take more club for the same distance.

Don't over-use a golf ball; once it begins to look a bit battered or has too many scratches either throw it away or put it in the practice bag. Never use old golf balls for putting practice though.

Golf equipment is expensive. You should have it tailored to your needs rather than buying the first set you see. You must then look after it. It will pay dividends in your score.